YOU CAN'T HAVE YOUR CAKE

AND EAT IT TOO

A Program for Controlling Bulimia

by

Lillie Weiss, Ph.D.
Arizona State University, Tempe

Melanie Katzman, Ph.D.
New York Hospital, Cornell Medical Center —
Westchester Division
Institute of Behavior Therapy in New York City

Sharlene Wolchik, Ph.D.
Arizona State University, Tempe

Published by
R & E PUBLISHERS
Post Office Box 2008
Saratoga, California 95070

Library of Congress Card Catalog Number
85-63016

I.S.B.N.
0-88247-750-1

TABLE OF CONTENTS

Appendices

LIST OF FIGURES

LIST OF TABLES

ACKNOWLEDGEMENTS

We would like to thank the many people who have helped us in the writing and publication of this book. First and foremost, we are indebted to the many women who have participated in our treatment program who have shared so freely of themselves.

We also thank Dr. Paul Karoly, Director of Clinical Training, Department of Psychology, at Arizona State University, for all of his help in getting this book published. We are very appreciative of his efforts and of his helpful suggestions.

Thanks also goes to Dr. Alex Zautra, Director of the Psychology Treatment Center at Arizona State University, and to the rest of the staff there for their support of the program. We thank Wendy, Gina and Judy for their assistance. We also thank Fran Beynon for her hard work in this program and for typing the manuscript.

Special thanks goes to Russell Macowsky for his legal assistance. We are indebted to him for all of his hard work on our manuscript when he had so much of his own work to do. We appreciate all of your help, Russell. We also thank our families for their support and encouragement.

PREFACE

Did you know that at least four out of every hundred college-aged females binge and purge regularly? That an even larger number of females have a very disturbed eating pattern? If you are someone who binges regularly or you binge and follow that by either vomiting, taking laxatives or diuretics, or starving yourself afterwards, or know someone who does, this book can serve as an educational and self-help guide. It can also be used by psychotherapists who are helping women with eating disorders. If you are like many women who regularly binge, you may feel that you are all alone with your "secret." You may be embarrassed or ashamed. You may be feeling out of control. Or you may know others in your situation and have even told your friends or family about your eating habits but still have no idea what to do about them. We are writing this book to share with you some information about bulimia and to give you tools that will help you gain control over your eating habits and behavior.

INTRODUCTION

*And if thou hast been forced to eat, arise, go forth,
vomit, and thou shalt have rest.*[1]

The consumption of large quantities of food followed by purging, once practiced in Biblical and ancient Roman times, has recently begun to receive renewed attention. Many articles have appeared recently both in the popular and professional literature describing this behavior. In 1980, the term bulimia, literally "ox hunger," was included as a diagnostic entity by the American Psychiatric Association.[2] Its features include rapid consumption of a large quantity of food in a short period of time followed by attempts to counteract this by self-induced vomiting, laxative abuse or extreme dietary restriction.

Although bulimia has been considered a rare disorder[3], recent studies suggest increased frequency in both clinical and college samples. Studies suggest that 4% to 19% of college-aged women[4,5,6,7] and 2% of older or nonstudent populations[8] are bulimic.

The eating habits of women who suffer from bulimia are more than just a nuisance. Bulimic women describe their eating pattern as very disruptive of their daily lives, causing them interference in their relationships, their jobs and their school performance.[9,10,11,12] In addition, many medical and psychological problems can develop as a result of this eating pattern.[13,14,15,16,17]

Although attention has been given to the problems associated with bulimia, there is very little written on its treatment. Existing treatment has focused primarily on the modification of eating habits rather than on the personality characteristics that may coexist with bulimia.[18,19]

1

How we came to write this book

Several years ago, we became interested in understanding how bulimia developed so that we could design a treatment program to help binge-purgers. Although much was postulated and written about the personality characteristics of bulimic women, no research was done to actually compare them with other women. We wanted to see how bulimic women were different from binge eaters and non-binge eaters. We studied 80 undergraduate students from A.S.U. and found differences between bulimics, binge eaters and controls. We found out that in comparison to controls, bulimics were more depressed, and had lower self-esteem, worse feelings about their bodies, higher self-expectations, and a higher need for approval than the non-bulimic women. What our results suggested was that treatment for bulimic women should extend beyond the disturbed eating pattern.[20]

Other research also suggests that bulimic women suffer from depression, low self-esteem, poor body image, perfectionistic tendencies, and a high need for approval[21,22], as well as difficulty in handling negative emotional states as anger or anxiety.[23,24,25,26] In addition, bulimic women were found to set unrealistic goals for thinness.[27] Despite the awareness of these clinical features associated with bulimia, no treatment program for this eating disorder has systematically addressed them in its approach.

We decided to develop a treatment program for bulimia based on those research findings. We developed a seven week self-enhancement program. Each session was designed to address one of the clinical features found to have been associated with bulimia. While we used behavior modification to help the bulimic gain control over her dysfunctional eating pattern, most of the attention was on developing new competencies rather than on the binge-purge cycle itself. We developed a treatment packet for each session consisting of reading materials, exercises and homework for that particular session. It was intended to be used as a workbook and as a self-help guide for maintenance after termination of the program. We have used this program with groups and individuals, with encouraging results.[28] Our findings have suggested that following the end of treatment, bulimic women reduced the frequency of bingeing and purging by over two-thirds of what it was at the beginning of treatment. They also showed improvement in body image, self-esteem and depression.

We were very encouraged by these results and further refined and expanded our program. Our purpose in writing this book is to share our program with you so that you can use it to help you with your problem.

How to use this book

Although this book is designed as a self-help guide, it can be most effective if you are working together with a trained psychotherapist. The structure of the book follows the general structure of the group therapy program. By reading about the experiences of other women, you may gain a clearer perspective of your own experiences. Each chapter covers a week of the seven week program which addresses a particular topic. At the end of each chapter there are homework assignments to do for that particular week. We have also included a daily binge-purge diary to help you become aware of your eating habits so that you can change them.

This book is intended to be a workbook with space allotted for you to write your thoughts, impressions and answers to exercises. The best way to use it is to read one chapter a week and do the exercises in it one week at a time. Or you may wish to read the whole book first and then go back and review each chapter, doing the exercises on a weekly basis. You may want to go at your own rate, of course, but you will get the most out of this book if you don't skip any of the exercises.

Just reading the contents of the book will have little effect without doing the homework exercises. The strategies we discuss deserve to be tested and tried. Throughout the book, we have left space for you to *record* your answers to questions. The recording is important, even if it may be time-consuming. At the end of each chapter, we have provided a page for you to write any notes you wish to yourself.

Whom this book is for

This book is for you if you are a bulimic or a binge-purger. If you binge regularly and then purge, whether by fasting, vomiting, exercise, taking laxatives or diuretics, you will find this book very beneficial. You are a binge eater if your have an uncontrollable urge to eat large quantities of high caloric food in a short period of time and feel bad about yourself after a binge. You are not a binge eater if you have a large appetite or occasionally eat second or third helpings. Although bulimia is defined in the DSM III, there is still some ambiguity as to what exactly constitutes a binge and what bingeing "regularly" means.

This book is not for you if you are an anorexic because the dynamics of anorexic women differ from those of bulimics. Although anorexics may engage in purging behavior as a means of controlling weight, they frequently define a binge as anything they put in their mouth. There are many differences between anorexics and

3

bulimics which we will discuss later in this book. Suffice it to say that if you are an anorexic, this book is not for you.

WEEK ONE

EDUCATION AND OVERVIEW

Take a few minutes to ask yourself why you are starting this program at this time. What do you hope to get out of it? When women first come to our program, we typically ask them what they hope to accomplish for themselves. Your reasons for tackling this problem now could be similar to some of the reasons given by the women who have participated in our program. Alice, a pretty, popular, verbal college student expressed it this way: "I am so tired of spending my whole life around this. It is time I got on with my life and not spend all my energy and time thinking about food." Others echoed this sentiment. "I want to be normal. I want to have a normal feeling about food," said Carla, another attractive, married woman who binged regularly. "I am too busy. I just don't have time in my life for this habit," said Doris. "It takes up all my thoughts and energy."

Together with wanting to get on with their lives and put food in its proper perspective, women also joined our program because they realized they could not stop this habit by themselves. "Every time I go for a few days or weeks without bingeing, I think I have this problem licked. But whom am I kidding? The next time I get stressed or break up with my boyfriend, it starts all over again," said Rhoda, an attractive, bright woman in her twenties who described her eating habits as cyclical. Others voiced the same concerns. "I've tried many times to stop and I'm really 'good' for a few days and then I start all over again. I'll look in a mirror and feel fat, and the next thing I know it's starting all over again," said another woman.

One of the biggest reasons for women to embark on this program was their experiencing a lack of control in their lives. They felt that their eating habits were controlling them. Many felt depressed and guilty about their behavior and that they were not in charge of their lives. In fact, depression was an accompanying part of this behavior for most women. "Help!" This seemed to be the cry that

5

was voiced over and over, in their words and actions, "Help me gain some control." Almost all of the women expressed a need to feel more in control as one of their major reasons for participating in the program.

"I am so tired of having to hide," said Alice. "It is such a nuisance. This is my own awful 'secret,' and I have to constantly make sure that nobody knows about it. I make all kinds of excuses for being alone so that nobody can see me 'pig out.' And I have to lie and scheme about where the money is going for all that food." Anna could relate to that very well: "The closest person in my life is my boyfriend. Yet I have to constantly make excuses and sneak out and lie so he won't discover my 'secret.' If he ever found out, I'd die. Yet how can I ever be close to him if I'm always hiding?" The feeling of "hiding," of having to keep a major part of their lives hidden, is a significant stressor for most of the women.

In addition, the practical financial and medical problems associated with bulimia have prompted many women to seek help. Diana, an attractive woman who majored in nutrition, realized some of the health hazards of her eating habits but sought help after she had nine thousand dollars' worth of dental bills from all of the induced vomiting. "I know about all the health problems of bulimia," said Alice, "but seeing someone who is actually having dental problems makes it real for me." Women mentioned other health problems that motivated them to come for treatment at this time. "I feel tired all the time now, and I have aches and pains," said Candy. "I know it's related to my eating habits, but I'm afraid to go for a checkup." "I used laxatives," said Rhoda, "but they really caused some terrible problems. I ruined my insides completely." Some women were very upset by the throat blisters that were the direct result of induced vomiting. In addition, they were spending all of their money for food. "I have so little money," said Doris, a young, vivacious college student. "How can I explain to my parents where all the money is going?"

All the women shared their reasons for wanting to change their eating habits. "You know," said Alice, summing it up, "I really want to change. I am tired of this burden. I want to go on with my life. But why haven't I so far? Maybe *I just don't know how*." Alice may have been speaking for the rest of the group when she said she really didn't know how.

Look at your reasons for wanting to change your behavior. Can you relate to any of the women in the group? Maybe you too want to get on with your life. Maybe right now you just don't know how. We'd like to teach you how by giving you some tools that have worked for other women, but we'd also like to caution you to set some realistic expectations for change. Don't start this program with

6

the goal that you will stop bingeing and purging completely after seven weeks. Many bulimic women are perfectionistic and set very high, if not impossible, goals for themselves. Then they get depressed and disappointed in themselves if they don't attain these goals. This leads to further bingeing, and a vicious cycle continues. Don't tell yourself you'll never binge again. A more realistic goal would be that you will reduce the frequency of your bingeing and purging. You may eliminate it completely —many have — but do not start out with such high expectations which only lead to frustration if not accomplished right away.

Although your goals may have to do with your eating behavior, the emphasis of this program is on *feelings*. Other goals for you would be to feel better about yourself and to be more in charge of your life. This is really a book about coping. Our program is to help you learn other, more constructive, ways of coping.

The structure of this book follows the general structure of the group therapy program. As we said before, each chapter covers a particular topic that has been found in the research to be associated with bulimia. Although we will pay attention to your eating habits and ask you to keep a daily food diary throughout the duration of this program, the main emphasis will be on teaching you other ways of coping so that you can take charge of your life.

One of the main goals for this particular week will be to give you some information on bulimia — what it is and what it isn't. We will also give you a chance to experience some of your feelings through the experiences of other women. In later weeks, we will discuss other associated psychological features shared by many bulimic women. We view the excessive eating as a means of coping, and we will explore together other ways of coping that can work for you. We have also found that bulimic women are more depressed, have lower self-esteem and expect more of themselves than other women do. We will explore these behaviors in detail and help you change your expectations and thinking about yourself so that you can start to like yourself more. Bulimic women were also frequently found to have difficulty expressing anger constructively. As one of our women put it, "I literally end up swallowing my anger and then spitting it up." We hope to help you understand and express anger in constructive ways. Almost all of the women we talked to, bulimic or not, have been conditioned to be slim and most feel that they are not living up to society's expectations of what a "perfect woman" is. We will talk about how to deal with societal pressures to be thin and how to become comfortable with our bodies, regardless of our shape and size. Finally, we will review your progress and prepare you for possible relapses.

This book is intended to be a workbook with space allotted for you to write your thoughts, impressions and answers to questions. Since it is a workbook, we expect you to *work*! It may be tempting to skip a chapter or not do some exercises because you don't have the time or things may be going well or even because you are feeling discouraged, but we urge you to do every exercise if you wish to get the best results.

Imagine that you are sitting with a group of women who binge and purge regularly. How would you feel? Would you feel relieved that you are not alone? Would you feel embarrassed? Would you feel that you can finally talk about your "secret?" The women attending our groups felt all of these. In a group, it was comforting to participate through the experiences of others, just as we urge you to do through this book. Many women experienced hope as they saw others change their eating habits. As one woman put it, "If she can do it, I can do it." For others, it was a relief to finally be able to share their feelings and be understood. "Every day I tell myself that I will be 'good.' And I try, I really try, then I start to study, and I suddenly get this uncontrollable urge and I don't know what happens. Then I feel so ashamed, so depressed, and I tell myself it will never happen again. But then it does and I feel more and more out of control," said Doris. Others nod because they have felt the same way at some time or other.

"I tell my friends that I binge but I don't think anyone really understands or knows how much I eat. I get so disgusted with myself."

"My parents know about this. They think I have stopped but I can't bear to let them know I haven't. I feel so guilty for letting them down."

"My husband tells me just to eat when I'm hungry. It's easy for him to say. Nobody can really understand what it's like for me."

These feelings of shame, disgust, guilt or the fact that nobody can really understand them occur for most bulimics. They are relieved to be able to express their feelings and learn that they are not alone.

Women also expressed feelings about societal pressures to be thin. "Every time you open a magazine," said Alice, "you see these wonderful gourmet recipes on the one hand and then you see these skinny models on the other, and you feel you're getting two messages. You always feel deprived." Many women, like Alice, get angry that they couldn't become like the skinny model in the magazines. All expressed their frustration with the difficulty of staying slim. "I think of food all the time," said Doris, "they say 'men lust after women, and women lust after food.' That's certainly true in my case." The frustration of wanting to be model-slim on the one hand and the hunger for good food on the other frequently results in the binge-purge cycle for many women. It's a way to have your cake and eat it too — or is it?

Let's explore a few facts about bulimia first. What is it? Bulimia is a name to describe a combination of thoughts and actions. These include:

1. an urge to eat large quantities of food in short periods of time (binges)
2. vomiting, exercising, fasting or the use of laxatives or water pills after a binge
3. repeated attempts to lose weight and frequent fluctuations in weight
4. bingeing in private, stopping when someone comes home
5. eating foods that are high in calories and require little preparation
6. feeling bad about yourself after a binge
7. feeling depressed about your eating habits

Who has it? Bulimia occurs most often in college-aged women, although many older females engage in this behavior. Women who are perfectionistic about their bodies and their lives (high achievers) often begin this cycle at about age 18. The research suggests that bulimic women suffer from depression, low self-esteem, poor feelings about their bodies, perfectionistic tendencies, and a high need for approval, as well as difficulty in handling negative emotional states such as anger. Bulimic women also set unrealistic goals for thinness. Bulimia is becoming increasingly common among college-aged women. Studies suggest that 4% to 19% of college-aged women demonstrate these behaviors.

Bulimia and anorexia nervosa have often been confused with each other. There are actually many differences between the two, although some bulimic women may have a history of anorexia nervosa. The bulimic woman is usually of normal weight, whereas the anorexic is at least 25% below normal. Most anorexics generally starve as a means of controlling weight, occasionally engaging in bingeing and purging behavior, unlike the bulimic who primarily binges and purges. The onset for anorexia is in the early teens, whereas it is in the late teens or early twenties for bulimia. The bulimic, in addition, is more socially and sexually experienced than the anorexic. A disturbed body image is necessary for the diagnosis of anorexia but not for bulimia. Treatment for the anorexic can be in an inpatient or outpatient setting, whereas the bulimic frequently receives outpatient treatment.

Why do so many women engage in this type of eating behavior? Betty's story is typical. Like many other young women in their late teens and early twenties, Betty was influenced by societal pressures to be thin and started going on a series of diets. Her dieting became more extreme, and her efforts to perfect herself through dieting led to her first binge. She felt very guilty and full after this binge and became sick afterwards. She felt better after she vomited, and the next time she overate, she simply put her finger down her throat and got rid of all the extra calories. Betty felt she had discovered a way to eat and yet lose weight. However, she labeled herself as "abnormal" because of her new eating behavior. She became depressed because of her "secret" and continued to binge to help her cope with her depression. This led to further guilt and feeling bad about herself. Thus, a vicious cycle developed. Soon the binge-purge cycle and the accompanying depression became all-consuming for her, disrupting her life in many ways.

What are some of the advantages of the binge-purge cycle? On the surface, it appears that you can have your cake and eat it too. People think it's an "easy" way to eat and stay slim. As we discussed before, it is tempting to eat all those wonderful foods and still stay slim. However, bulimia has both psychological and physical disadvantages. The women in the program were all aware of the psychological consequences of bulimia. They felt out of control, depressed, embarrassed and guilty. The bulimic's guilty secret limits her social contacts and results in social isolation. The secret rituals associated with this behavior cause a disruption in her interpersonal relationships. The bulimic woman frequently has obsessive thoughts about food, and her thoughts and behaviors literally become an all-consuming part of her life. That was why so many women reported in one form or other that they "just wanted to get on with their lives."

The physical hazards of bulimia are also very serious. Although the bulimic woman originally engages in this behavior to become attractive, this may result in very unattractive physical features such as her teeth falling out. She may be slim but toothless. In addition, the stench from the vomiting can be repulsive to the bulimic and to those around her. Some other medical complications may follow, both from the bingeing and the purging. These include throat blisters, ruptured stomach and esophagus, kidney problems, rotten teeth, electrolyte imbalance, amenorrhea, anemia and other problems. We need to emphasize these complications because frequently bingeing and purging are glamorized, and many bulimic women who engage in this behavior because it appears to be an "easy" way to lose weight discover to their chagrin the heavy physical penalty they have to pay. As one woman put it, "I may look good on the outside but my insides are falling apart." An awareness of these physical hazards may help you reassess the price of this "easy" way to lose weight. Although many bulimics may feel that "this won't happen to me," they may discover to their horror and too late the heavy physical price they have paid for their behavior.

We have tried to present some of the facts about bulimia. Unfortunately, there are many misconceptions about it that have sprung up which have interfered with women seeking help and have led to feelings of hopelessness and depression. Maybe you have encountered some of these misconceptions yourself. When we asked the women in our program what they had heard about bulimia, there was a general embarrassed laughter. Then one woman said, "It's a disease." Another said, "It's a mental illness. My mother says people who have bulimia are crazy." Unfortunately, this popular view of bulimia as a mental illness contributes to the bulimic woman's feelings of inadequacy and causes her to feel worse about herself. This leads to her being even more secretive about her behavior because people will think she is crazy. In addition to the bulimic label, she labels herself "crazy," "abnormal" or "mentally ill." Although the term bulimia is listed by the American Psychiatric Association as a diagnostic entity, a woman who fits this description is no more "crazy" or "abnormal" than a woman who shows symptoms of depression. Labeling behavior a mental illness can have serious implications for treatment because the bulimic woman feels that this behavior is outside her control, that it is something she "catches" and that it won't go away. Our view is that bingeing and purging are habits, poor habits maybe, but behaviors that are *learned*, and if you can learn something, you can also *unlearn* it. If you look at your behavior, when you started to binge and purge, you may, like some of the other women, have learned this from others or you may have purged after a heavy meal and discovered how reinforcing that could be. At some point, you learned to use this method when you have felt anxious, stressed, depressed, lonely, or fat. You may not even remember how or when this behavior started. Many women say, "It's such a habit now." Or "What else is there to do when I come home?" Viewing the binge-purge cycle as learned behavior gives many women hope and the sense that this is something within their control.

A second common misconception about bulimia is that the bulimic woman has no control when she is around food, that "an uncontrollable urge" overtakes her, and before you know it, she has consumed several thousand calories. This brings to mind some of the novels and romance magazines depicting women being caught up in passion and succumbing to it, losing their virginity before they can say "boo." This myth takes the responsibility away from the behavior. Both overeating and engaging in sexual intercourse involve many conscious acts. It takes a deliberate act to open the refrigerator door or to take off your clothing to engage in sex. In both

11

cases, some extra planning is needed to set the scene for these behaviors to occur. Bulimics frequently plan their binges at a time when they are alone. They obviously have control because they will not binge when others are around or in certain other situations. It is important that you don't buy this myth and that you do take responsibility for your behavior. Otherwise, you will only feel more helpless and depressed.

Other irrational beliefs about bulimia have kept women from seeking help or changing their behavior. Newspapers and magazine articles have depicted bulimia as an intractably ingrained feature that has taken years to develop and may take years to eliminate. This creates some pessimism and keeps women from seeking help to change their behavior. They may wonder, "What's the use?" The truth is that women with a long history of bingeing and purging have stopped bingeing. This is important to bring out because a hope and a belief that you can change are an integral first step in your trying new coping responses.

Some women may be afraid to try new behaviors because they feel that if they stop bingeing and purging, they will have to change in other ways as well. "As long as I engage in this behavior," said Sally, "nothing much is really expected of me. I mean, really, what can you expect from someone who has so little control over her life? Having this habit keeps me from going out with others, keeps me broke, gives me a good excuse not to do well in school. . . ." We reassured Sally that giving up this habit meant giving up bingeing and purging, nothing more. She could continue to be as unsocial, disorganized and lazy as she wanted. Other women are afraid to find out that everything will not change once they change their eating habits. Judy was convinced that she had no friends because of her eating habits. She was afraid to discover that she may still be unpopular and lonely without that excuse.

All of these misconceptions are really excuses or cop-outs for not taking responsibility for our actions. Our basic philosophy is that every woman is responsible for her behavior and that by acting on this responsibility, she will feel more in charge of her life. In our groups, we ask women what types of cop-outs they may use. This is to help them identify them so that they can become aware of them in the future. We also ask women to call on each other's cop-outs. We do not help people by telling them what they want to hear. We can help them most by bringing their behavior to their awareness. When we ask group members what types of "cop-outs" they may use, they frequently respond, "not attending all of the sessions" or "feeling I'm doing so well, I don't need it." It may be tempting for you to skip some of the material. However, this is self-defeating.

"I may 'cop-out' by feeling none of this applies to me," said

Diana, a nutrition major who could teach us a course on healthy eating habits but who still denied that whatever she learned could apply to her.

Some women needed their "cop-outs" pointed out to them by the group. "I wonder if there may be some attention or prestige associated with being bulimic," Cathy suggested to Alice. Alice blushed but readily admitted, "You know, all my friends had 'a problem' — my best friend had an abortion, my other friend was dating a married man, everyone had something intriguing and interesting in their lives. I guess bulimia made me special and interesting."

The biggest "cop-outs" are those that imply a loss of responsibility such as "something just overtakes me" or "I don't even realize I'm doing it" or "I don't even try to throw up. It just happens."

Women who use laxatives to maintain their weight may cop-out by saying they will keep the laxatives in their purse ("I just won't use them") or "I'm not ready to throw out my laxatives yet." These women are really saying, "I want to continue bingeing and purging but I won't take the responsibility for that by saying it out loud." If you are saying that, then you will need to take responsibility for continuing the binge/purge cycle. For laxative users, an essential component of the program is throwing away the laxatives by the second session. If you do not want to do that by then, it would be advisable to discontinue the program and start only when you are ready. Otherwise, you are wasting your time.

Here are some common cop-outs:

"I've been doing this for so long. I can't change."
"Something just overtakes me."
"It's a habit."
"I don't even realize I'm doing it."
"I can't lose weight any other way."
"Once I start, I can't stop."
"This has been such a stressful week."
"I can't give up my laxatives yet."
"I can keep the laxatives; I just won't use them."
"I don't even try to throw up; it just happens."
"I'm going to throw up afterwards anyway, so I might as well eat whatever I want."

Which of these do you use?

What are some other cop-outs?

Before you begin

Before doing the homework for this program, take a few minute to take stock of where you are now by answering the following questions.

1. How often have you gone on an eating binge in the last month? Remember, a binge is *at least* 1200 calories and is usually high caloric food that is easily ingested._____

2. How often have you purged after bingeing in the last month by using either self-induced vomiting, laxatives, diuretics (pills that force urination) or severely restrictive diets?_____

3. What is the average caloric content of each binge?_____

4. How long does a binge last?_____

5. How many times in the last month have you eaten three meals a day?_____

6. How many times in the last month have you weighed yourself?_____

7. How many days in the last month have you gone without bingeing?_____

8. How many times in the last month have you done something else instead when you have felt the urge to binge?_____

   _____

9. Which statement best describes the way you feel about yourself?
   _____ I like myself very much
   _____ I like myself most of the time
   _____ I only like myself some of the time

14

_____ I don't like myself most of the time

_____ I hate myself

10. Which statement best describes the way you feel about your body?

         _____ I like and accept my body

         _____ I like my body most of the time

         _____ I only like my body some of the time

         _____ Most of the time I don't like my body

         _____ I hate my body

11. Which statement best describes your level of depression?

         _____ I am not depressed

         _____ I am mildly depressed

         _____ I am very depressed

         _____ At times I feel suicidal

12. What are my reasons for wanting to control my eating habits?

At the end of this program, refer back to your answers here to assess your progress and where you still need to go.

HOMEWORK

1. Review the information on bulimia in this chapter.

2. Look at the list of cop-outs. Circle the ones you use. What are some others? Review this list from time to time. If you are a laxative user, be prepared to throw out the laxatives by the second session. If you vomit after bingeing, make up your mind not to purge regardless of how much you eat because knowing that you will be purging afterwards serves as a cop-out and gives you permission to binge. Enlist the aid of a friend or your therapist to call you on your "cop-outs."

3. Start recording in the binge-purge diary at the end of this chapter. Record only your *binges* for week 1. Remember, a binge is a very large amount of food, usually several thousand calories. It is not five potato chips, or having that second or third helping. Put a *P* each time you purged after a binge; that is, each time you vomited or used laxatives or diuretics in an attempt to empty yourself of the food. Write down everything you ate during the binge, and your thoughts and feelings prior to eating. You don't need to fill out the alternative coping skills yet until the next session unless you can note some specific things you could have done instead of bingeing. Please record the total number of binges and purges for this week in the diary. We are aware that this diary may be difficult or embarrassing to fill out. However, it is easiest to change behavior when you can identify it. We are aware that for many women the act of writing down everything they eat during a binge is very difficult. Frequently, they will report that it takes too much time or they "forget." However, it has been our experience that only through accurate recording can women discover what triggers their binges. You may not be aware of what those feelings are at first but try to pay attention to what you are telling yourself before you binge. After a while, it will become easier for you to do so. Remember, you do not need to write down *everything* you eat that week, just your binges.

NOTES

WEEKLY BINGE DIARY

NAME_____ WEEK NO._____

	TIME	WHAT I ATE	FEELINGS AND THOUGHTS PRIOR TO EATING	ALTERNATIVE COPING SKILLS
MONDAY				
TUESDAY				
WEDNESDAY				
THURSDAY				

WEEKLY BINGE DIARY

NAME_____ WEEK NO._____

	TIME	WHAT I ATE	FEELINGS AND THOUGHTS PRIOR TO EATING	ALTERNATIVE COPING SKILLS
F R I D A Y				
S A T U R D A Y				
S U N D A Y				

TOTAL NUMBER OF BINGES THIS WEEK_____

TOTAL NUMBER OF PURGES THIS WEEK_____

WEEK TWO

EATING AS COPING: DEVELOPING ALTERNATIVE COPING STRATEGIES

Life itself is the proper binge.[1]

This chapter is about coping and finding other ways than food to deal with life. For most bingers, eating is a way of coping with stress. Here we are going to help you find some alternative coping skills. To learn how you are using bingeing as a way to cope, look at your binge diary this past week. What were your thoughts and feelings prior to eating? Can you identify a pattern?

"You know," said Carol, "it seems I eat just because I'm home alone. I don't even think about it. It's automatic. I go home, I'm alone, and that's a cue for me to eat. I don't know if you call it boredom or loneliness or what, but I just seem to do it when I'm home alone." Carol had quickly identified the cues that preceded her binge: being home alone and feeling bored or lonely. Once she recognized what precipitated her bingeing behavior, she quickly made some changes. "I decided that since I eat when I'm home alone before anybody else gets home, I would now go to the library to study instead of going home directly."

Donna, like many other college students, also binged when studying. "I think of all the work I have to do, and I sit down to study and all I can think about is food." Donna, unlike Carol, did not change the conditions that caused her to binge right away. She resisted studying at the library at first. "It's too far away," she said. "Besides, it seems like such a waste of time. I should be able to learn to study at home without bingeing." When it was pointed out to her that this hadn't worked for her, she started leaving the house when she was stressed. She was surprised to find that she cut down on her binges drastically. Donna, like many bulimic women, was very hard on herself and expected too much from herself by saying, "I *should*

19

be able to be home alone and not binge." Once she learned to make it easier for herself not to binge, she cut down on her binges dramatically.

The first step in developing alternative coping responses is to make it easier for yourself to develop new eating habits. Once you identify the cues that start you bingeing, you can quickly plan another coping mechanism that will make it simpler for you not to binge. The key word here is *planning* in advance what alternative coping skill you will use.

Carmela, a bright, efficient medical secretary and mother of two pre-schoolers, frequently binged after a long day at the office, which ended in a late staff meeting where drinks and hors d'oeuvres were served. She would manage to resist the temptation to eat this high caloric "junk food" at the meeting and get hungrier by the minute. She would come home late at night, feeling tired, hungry and weak. After watching her husband and children consume a high caloric dinner while she nibbled on a salad, she would binge when the rest of the family went to bed. Afterwards she would feel guilty and depressed for bingeing after being so "good" all day. Carmela, like many other women, was very perfectionistic and set impossible goals for herself. It was pointed out to her that it would be impossible for anyone to starve all day and not be hungry at night. She made plans to prevent the next binge by eating a nutritious but low caloric meal before the staff meeting so she would not have to feel hungry and faint throughout the meeting. Even though her work schedule was hectic, she was able to buy packets of cheese from the cafeteria nearby and eat those during the day. Other women with heavy schedules have found that having nutritious and filling food available, such as cheese and crackers or yogurt, can prevent the hunger that precipitates a binge.

Many women binge because they make the common mistake of starving themselves all day long and then feel extremely hungry in the evening. If your pattern is one of near starvation during the day, you are setting yourself up for a binge. Your body needs a certain amount of food and you can't fool it by not giving it the nutrients. When it's starved and you binge, your body is talking. One of the *best preventative measures* for an oncoming binge is to eat three meals a day.

We have talked of boredom and loneliness as well as excessive hunger from near starvation as being cues for a binge. What other thoughts and feelings do you have before bingeing? Diana, an attractive, slender woman in her 20's, said that looking in the mirror is generally a cue for her to start bingeing. "I look in the mirror and think 'I'm fat.' Then I figure what difference does it make if I eat or not — I'll always be fat — so I get depressed and start bingeing."

Janet, another slim, attractive woman, also said feeling fat precipitated a binge. "I'll go to a party or something, and I'll look at all those other women who are so much thinner than I am, and I'll compare myself to them. I'll get depressed and go home and binge." Joannie would feel fat after getting on the scale and finding out she hadn't lost much weight even though she had been so "good." She would think, "What's the use?" and give herself permission to binge. A first step for Joannie would be to get rid of her scale.

Besides feeling depressed about being "fat," women also identified feeling anxious before they binged. "This has been such a stressful week. I have so much on my mind, and I have just been so anxious, nervous that I'd lose my job, nervous about all the schoolwork I have, worried about money. So I eat so that I can forget about it and relax," said Jane. Eating seemed to serve the role of reducing the anxiety right away for Jane. However, it made her more upset and nervous later on. "How else can you relax?" we asked her. Jane came up with several other ways of relaxing, such as taking a bubble bath, calling a friend or going for a walk.

"I eat to avoid facing things," said Rhoda. "It's like everything in my life is out of control. I just don't want to think about it, so I eat, and that calms me down — at least right away." Underneath the avoidance, we could hear that Rhoda was depressed. She was feeling overwhelmed and rejected and food gave her that feeling of comfort that she craved. How else could she "nurture" herself? How else could she give herself a "treat" which she so badly needed right now? Rhoda was told to think of another way she could nourish herself. She decided to give herself a treat by splurging on some special cologne for herself and using it after a long and luxurious bubble bath.

Janet binged when she was angry. She recognized that bingeing regularly followed an argument, generally when she kept her feelings to herself and felt smoldered with resentment afterwards. She would then go and raid the refrigerator which would temporarily alleviate the hurt. Afterwards she would throw up which was like a "cleansing." Janet learned ways of expressing her anger more assertively and felt "cleansed" by letting it out rather than keeping it inside.

Anger, hurt, depression, nervousness, guilt, boredom. . .all of these feelings precipitate binges. When we look at all the different cues that lead to a binge, it is probably surprising that those are mainly emotional triggers. Can you identify your emotional triggers? What kinds of thoughts and feelings do you have before you binge? Before you eat, ask yourself, "What's eating me?"

Ironically, the only time hunger alone is a trigger for a binge is when the hunger is excessive and caused by near starvation, after being "good" all day and not giving the body what it needs. Many women do not feed their bodies because they do not realize how much they can really eat and not gain weight. They feel a slice of bread or a piece of cheese will make them obese overnight. Diana, a nutrition major, stated she ate normal meals during the day which consisted of black coffee for breakfast and an apple for lunch! In addition, many women have no idea what should be a normal weight for them and strive for unrealistic weights that do not fit their heights or bone structure.

Although the main thrust of this book is on feelings and coping, we would like to present some basic nutritional facts because an insufficient familiarity with these lead women to binge. Learning healthy and regular eating habits is one of the basic coping skills.

Following is the 1983 Metropolitan Height and Weight Table for women.[2]

1983 METROPOLITAN HEIGHT AND WEIGHT TABLE*

Height		Small	Medium	Large
Feet	Inches	Frame	Frame	Frame
4	10	102-111	109-121	118-131
4	11	103-113	111-123	120-134
5	0	104-115	113-126	122-137
5	1	106-118	115-129	125-140
5	2	108-121	118-132	128-143
5	3	111-124	121-135	131-147
5	4	114-127	124-138	134-151
5	5	117-130	127-141	137-155
5	6	120-133	130-144	140-159
5	7	123-136	133-147	143-163
5	8	126-139	136-150	146-167
5	9	129-142	139-153	149-170
5	10	132-145	142-156	152-173
5	11	135-148	145-159	155-176
6	0	138-151	148-162	158-179

*Metropolitan Life Insurance Company, Health and Safety Education Division Weights at ages 25-59 based on lowest mortality. Weight in pounds according to frame (in indoor clothing weighing 3 lbs. for women; shoes with 1" heels)

Find your recommended weight from the table by looking for your height with 1" heels. What is your reaction when you see what your weight should be? Most women are surprised by this table and set their ideal weight at least 10 or 20 pounds below these norms. Study this table carefully. You may be within the appropriate weight for your height. When Rhoda looked at this table, she wondered if she hadn't been putting excessive pressure on herself to be thin. "I was always happy at 130 pounds but I keep trying to be 110 pounds. Now this table tells me I'm in the right weight range all along. Maybe I should just leave well enough alone and not put so much pressure on myself to be model slim." Rhoda's desire to be "model slim" was echoed by others. Where does this desire come from? Society may condition us that 103 pounds is the only way to be. However, that is neither healthy nor ideal for most of us, and trying to live up to some unrealistic image of thinness can only cause frustration and depression.

In addition to setting unrealistic goals for thinness, many women have no idea how much they can eat and maintain their weight. They feel that a sandwich or a restaurant meal will make them balloon overnight. We would like to give you some basic information to help you determine how to best control your weight. Here are some "fat facts."

Fat Facts

How many calories can I eat and still maintain my weight?

Pick your current weight from the Metropolitan Height and Weight Table and multiply this by 12. That is how many calories you can eat and not gain weight. For example, if you weigh 110 pounds, multiply 110 by 12, which means you can eat 1320 calories daily and still maintain your weight.

If your weight is 124 pounds (which is the lower end of the scale for a 5'4" women of medium frame), you can eat up to 1488 calories daily and not gain weight.

About how much weight is that?

Below are some sample menus to maintain weights of 110 pounds (1320 calories daily) and 124 pounds (1488 calories daily).

1320 calories daily =

breakfast: 1 egg, 1 English muffin, jam, orange juice

lunch: turkey sandwich with cheese and mayonnaise, chips on the side

dinner: 4 oz. chicken, baked potato, salad, vegetable, apple

You can eat all of this and still maintain your weight! You do not need to starve yourself to do so. 1320 calories is also: 2 bags of M and M's, 5 Chips Ahoy cookies, 1 dish of ice cream, 1 piece of pie.

1488 calories daily=

> **breakfast:** fried egg, 2 strips bacon, slice toast
> **lunch:** roast beef sandwich, salad with dressing, orange
> **dinner:** broiled sirloin steak, baked potato, green beans with butter, ½ cantaloupe

Remember, you can eat this much and maintain your weight without any activity. If you exercise, you can eat much more. 1488 calories is also: apple pie, 2 doughnuts, chocolate ice cream sundae, cheese cake; or —candy bar, chocolate cake, eclair, 3 chocolate chip cookies.

How many calories can I eat and still lose one pound a week? Two pounds?

One pound of fat is equal to 3200 calories. Reduce your intake by 3200 and you lose a pound. Reduce intake by 450 calories a day and lose one pound a week. Reduce intake by 900 calories a day and lose two pounds a week. So, if you want to weigh 110 pounds, you can eat 870 calories a day and still lose one pound a week as you head toward your goal.

What if I want to lose weight faster?

Increasing your activity level means that your body needs more calories to maintain your weight. Increasing activity without increasing eating means you will lose weight faster. Regular exercise helps you reduce and stay slim.

How do I know if I'm looking slimmer?

Getting on the scale daily is not helpful. What you weigh on a particular day is not necessarily an indicator of weight gain or weight loss. At times, especially before your period and midway through your cycle, water retention may be the cause for your weight to go up. Also, inches lost through exercise may not be reflected on the scale. Remember: muscle weighs more than fat.

By the time you have read this far, you may have gained some understanding of what emotional and situational triggers precede your binges. We also hope that you are learning some basic facts about maintaining your weight. Although this book focuses mainly on feelings and coping, knowledge of basic nutrition is important. We cannot stress how important it is to eat three meals a day as a basic coping skill because starvation and its accompanying hunger and feelings of deprivation invariably lead to binges. We know that starvation alone can lead to an increased interest and preoccupation with food, and bulimia can be a natural consequence. In the long run, you lose weight much faster by developing a regular pattern.

Another way to control your bingeing is to make up your mind that you are not going to purge after a binge, *no matter how much you have eaten*. If you are a laxative user, now is the time to throw out your laxatives. If you generally vomit after a large meal, you may be using purging as a cop-out to continue eating. You may be saying, "I might as well overeat since I'm going to throw up afterwards." Many women cut down on the size of their binges once they know they are not going to get rid of the food.

What are some other coping skills that will work for you? We'd like to use an acronym *I COPE* to illustrate some basic coping skills. *I* stands for identifying stress, and each of the letters in the word *COPE* stands for a different stress skill: *C*ommunication, *O*rganization, *P*erception and *E*nhancement. Let's give you an example: Suppose that you are sitting at home preparing for a test when you head for the refrigerator. The first step is *identifying your stress*. We have asked you to do that in the binge diary. How do you know you are stressed? What thoughts and feelings do you have? You may be feeling anxious, telling yourself you are not prepared for the test, you may feel tired or cranky, or you may even be shaking. Each one of us has her own way of experiencing stress. Once you identify your feeling, then you can choose a number of stress skills besides bingeing to get rid of that knot in your stomach. You can use the coping response of *communication* and call a friend to tell her how you feel. "Talking it out" can help you feel better. Or you can use *organization* to cope. You can organize your time and decide what you will study. This will help you feel more prepared and less stressed. You can also change your *perception* of the situation. Instead of seeing this exam as a monumental task, you can remind yourself that it is only one small part of your total education. You may change your thinking about it from "I'm going to fail" to "I've done well in the past and there's no reason why I shouldn't pass this test." You can also use *enhancement* skills to help you cope. We always cope with stress better when we enhance ourselves. Getting a good night's sleep, eating right and relaxing can help you be more alert and cope better with the pressures.

Study the I COPE concept and record in the spaces: How do you know when you are stressed? Which stress skills could you use more of?

I COPE

*I*dentifying stress

*C*ommunication
*O*rganization
*P*erception
*E*nhancement

IDENTIFYING STRESS
How do you know when you are stressed?

COMMUNICATION SKILLS
Assertiveness: expressing your needs and saying "no"
Listening: tuning into other people's feelings
Making contact: seeking out friends who support you
Which of these skills could I use more of?

ORGANIZATION SKILLS
Pacing: choosing the rhythm that works for you
**Prioritizing: setting priorities and deciding how you spend your
time**
Planning: setting goals and making progress toward them
Which of these skills could I use more of?

PERCEPTION SKILLS
Re-labeling: changing the way you think about some things
Letting go: accepting what you can't change
Whisper: giving yourself gentle, positive messages
Which of these skills could I use more of?

ENHANCEMENT SKILLS
Taking care of your body: through eating, sleep and exercise
Gentleness: treating yourself kindly and gently
**Relaxation: taking time to relax through breathing, meditation,
and other ways**
Which of these skills could I use more of?

We said that one basic coping skill is changing the way you perceive a situation or think about it. Our thoughts about the situation rather than the situation itself affect how we feel and how we act. For example, a job change can be thought of as either a catastrophe or a challenge by different people, and they will react enthusiastically or hopelessly to it depending on their perceptions. To find out how we think about a particular situation, we need to listen carefully to what we are telling ourselves about it. This is very important when it comes to how we think about food and our eating behavior. Look again at the thoughts you wrote down in your binge diary. What do you tell yourself before a binge? Do you tell yourself that you are so nervous that you just have to eat? That you are not

27

losing fast enough? That you can't stop thinking about food? That you just can't control yourself? These thoughts are negative monologues and give us permission to binge. It is important to recognize these negative monologues and replace them with more appropriate ones.

Joannie was surprised to discover that her negative monologue went like this: "I'm going on a diet tomorrow. This is my last chance to eat." This gave her permission to binge because she told herself that if she didn't eat now, she would not eat for a long time. She changed the monologue to a more appropriate one: "If I'm going on a diet tomorrow, bingeing will only make me heavier and I'll have more weight to lose. If I don't binge now, I'll be rewarded by losing weight faster."

Mary gave herself permission to binge and purge by telling herself: "If I gain one pound, I'll go on and gain a hundred pounds." She recognized how irrational this sounded, and when she had that thought again, she told herself: "There I go again with my crazy thinking."

Our negative thinking about food extends to many areas and makes it easier for us to binge. We have compiled a list of statements that women frequently tell themselves. They are listed in the table on the next few pages, "Changing The Way You Think." We have replaced each of these statements, or negative monologues, with a more appropriate monologue.

Study the table carefully and circle the negative monologues you use. How can you change those?

Are there other thoughts you have that lead to bingeing? Write these down:

How can you replace those with a more appropriate monologue?
Write one appropriate monologue down.

CHANGING THE WAY YOU THINK

Negative Monologues	Appropriate Monologues
"I want to lose weight fast."	"I'll gain the pounds right back if I don't change my eating habits."
"If I gain one pound, I'll go on and gain twenty pounds."	"This is crazy all-or-nothing thinking."
"Gaining ten pounds would push me over the edge."	"There I go again with my crazy thinking."
"I've discovered an easy way to diet. I can eat everything and not have to count calories."	"This is an easy way to die! My teeth will fall out, my stomach will rupture, my kidneys will fail and my esophagus will get inflamed."
"Eating sweets is the only way to give myself a real treat. It's the one way that I know to cheer myself up."	"I can use the time bingeing and throwing up to have fun in other ways."
"The only way to relax while studying is to nibble."	"There are other ways to relax. Why not call a friend or take a walk?"
"I have had a terrible day. I think I'll cheer myself up with a snack."	"Think how terrible I will feel afterwards."
"I was good all day. I will just have a little pick now."	"There's no such thing as a 'little pick' when your stomach is empty. Next time don't starve yourself — that's not being good."
"I don't feel like doing anything at the moment. I'll make me something to eat."	"I'm really not hungry. Bingeing will make me feel bad afterwards. Why don't I do something else instead?"
"I'm so tense. If I eat this bag of cookies and throw up, I'll feel better."	"Nonsense. Vomiting makes you feel gross. There are other ways to relax."

"I'm all alone now. There's my chance to eat."

"Nonsense. This is not the only time to eat. If I eat sensibly, I could enjoy my meals with others."

"It's there. It's free. Why let it go to waste?"

"I'm going to throw it up anyway. Why bother going through the trouble of eating and vomiting?"

"Well, I blew it with that dough-nut. There goes my diet."

"Why should one sweet blow it for me?"

"If I eat a candy, it will instantly be converted into stomach fat."

"No one gets fat from one sweet."

"If I eat one cookie, I'll have to eat the whole box."

"You can enjoy one cookie but eating the whole box won't feel any better."

"I just can't control myself."

'Of course I can control myself. I control myself too much."

"Eating is the only way I can feel in control."

"Nonsense! Look how many prob-lems it has caused already. This is crazy thinking again!"

"Eating is disgusting. Now I feel like a cow."

"Eating is natural. If you eat naturally, you don't need to feel like a cow."

"If I can't control my eating, I'm not worth anything."

"I am more than my eating habits."

"I have this gross bulge in my stomach. I better vomit it off."

"Vomit is grosser. Everyone's stom-ach extends after eating. Let the food digest and the bulge will disappear."

"I'm going to vomit until I'm thin and pretty."

"Continuous vomiting will make my teeth fall out — that is not very attractive."

"If I'm thin and beautiful, then my boyfriend will want to be with me more."

"I'm always so worried that he'll discover my 'secret.' I don't even let myself enjoy the time with him. I should just be myself."

31

"I can't stop thinking about food."	"Whenever I find myself thinking about food, I can change the topic to some other pleasant experience."
"I just want to taste, no need to cut off a portion."	"When I eat standing in front of the refrigerator, I can't tell how much I'm eating. I'll just cut myself a piece and sit down and enjoy it."

Remember, if you want to change your eating behavior, change the way you think about it. A change in thinking leads to a change in behavior.

We said before that changing your eating behavior involves some planning beforehand. Once you have identified the emotional triggers that precipitate a binge, it is important to plan some specific strategies to combat these, some "tricks" that you can plan in advance rather than at the last minute. We have included a list of strategies for confronting an oncoming binge to give you some ideas.

STRATEGIES FOR CONFRONTING AN ONCOMING BINGE

1. *EAT THREE MEALS A DAY.* Include a carbohydrate food, such as fruits, grains, bread, pasta, at every meal. This will help cut down on the carbohydrate deprivation that often leads to bingeing.

2. *PUT SOMETHING SOUR IN YOUR MOUTH.* A slice of lemon or lime, a dill pickle. The sourness will affect your taste buds and may eliminate a craving for sweets.

3. *CHOOSE FRUIT OR JUICE* or just the tiniest quantity necessary of a sugar food to get you through the crisis.

4. *TAKE YOUR TIME.* Eat your food *slowly*, sitting down, putting your knife and fork down after every bite.

5. *FREEZE ORANGE OR GRAPEFRUIT JUICE* in ice-cube trays for a quick fix when you feel yourself going up the wall.

6. *TAKE PREVENTATIVE ACTION.* Do something active like scrubbing the floor or writing a letter. Keep at it for at least an hour, sipping water to make you feel full. Usually the urge to eat will pass.

7. *BRUSH YOUR TEETH* with flavored toothpaste, or gargle and rinse with a strong mouthwash.

8. *KEEP "SNOWBALLS" IN YOUR FREEZER.* Make them out of crushed ice and diet soda frozen in little paper cups. Eat slowly with a dessert spoon.

9. *SUCK ON AN ICE CUBE.*

10. *SET A TIMER FOR 10 MINUTES* and keep busy. When it goes off, ask yourself whether you are still truly hungry. If you are, go and eat, but choose an unfavorite food with few calories.

11. *EXERCISE.* Take a brisk walk or a bike ride or jog in place. It will remove you from temptation and depress your appetite.

12. *POLISH YOUR FINGERNAILS.* Two coats. By the time the polish dries, you probably won't be hungry anymore.

13. *GET ALL X-RATED FOOD OUT OF YOUR HOUSE.* If you must have them for the family, lock them in a closet and give the key to someone else.

14. *STORE LEFTOVERS* in individual portions in foil, then push them to the back of the refrigerator. Better still, throw them out.

15. *COOK JUST ENOUGH FOOD* to fill your plate only once.

16. *NEVER SERVE FAMILY-STYLE.*

17. *SERVE YOURSELF* meals on small plates.

18. *DO NOT GO FOOD SHOPPING HUNGRY.* Shop after a satisfying meal. Go only once a week and stick to a list.

19. *CHEW GUM WHILE YOU COOK.* To taste, you must deliberately remove the gum.

20. *EAT IN ONE PLACE ONLY* — sitting down at a table. No food goes into the living room, den, bedroom. Ever.

21. *WHEN WATCHING TELEVISION*, keep your hands busy.

22. *PLAN YOUR WEEKENDS AND EVENINGS TO KEEP YOU*

BUSY.

23. ***DRINK A TALL GLASS OF WATER*** about half an hour before a meal. Sip it slowly and it will fill you up so you'll eat less.

24. ***EAT A SALAD*** before your meal to take the steam out of your appetite. Or chew celery stalks, cucumber sticks, or carrots.

25. ***EAT FOODS THAT REQUIRE A LOT OF CHEWING*** like fresh vegetables or some unbuttered popcorn before a meal. This satisfies the desire for texture and helps tire your jaw muscles.

26. ***DRINK ICE WATER WITH YOUR MEALS.***

27. ***DON'T GIVE UP YOUR MOST FAVORITE FOODS*** — just eat less of them. Be sure the number of calories is within your total allowance, cutting back on other foods to make room for the specials.

28. ***NEVER FINISH A MEAL IN LESS THAN 20 MINUTES.*** That's how long it takes for the physiological signals of satiety to travel from your stomach to your brain.

29. ***THROW OUT YOUR LAXATIVES.***

30. ***REMIND YOURSELF THAT YOU WILL NOT PURGE REGARDLESS OF HOW MUCH YOU EAT.***

31. ***DO NOT WEIGH YOURSELF DAILY.*** Remember, your weight fluctuates on a daily basis and at certain times of the month you may be retaining water. Frequently, getting on the scale is a cue for a binge. Better yet, get rid of your scale.

32. ***CLEAN OUT YOUR CLOSET AND THROW AWAY THOSE SIZE 2 OR 3 CLOTHES YOU HAVE NOT BEEN ABLE TO GET INTO.*** This only makes you more depressed and encourages you to set unrealistic goals.

33. ***READ THE NEWSPAPER.***

34. ***CALL A FRIEND.***

35. ***TAKE A WALK.***

36. *LISTEN TO MUSIC.*

37. *TAKE A WARM SHOWER OR A HOT BATH.*

38. *WRITE IN A DIARY.*

39. *WRITE A LETTER TO A FRIEND.*

40. *DO SOME YOGA, MEDITATION, OR OTHER FORM OF RELAXATION.*

41. *PAMPER YOURSELF WITH A FACIAL.*

42. *GO TO THE MOVIES.*

Study these strategies. Which of those do you think would work for you? Circle those that seem to fit for you most. Are there other strategies or "gimmicks" you can use? Write those down.

HOMEWORK

1. We hope that by this time you have a good idea of what triggers your binges and have identified your thoughts and feelings prior to bingeing. You also have looked at other alternative coping responses. We would like you now to review this chapter and what you have written and to develop your own list of coping behaviors. In what other ways can you give yourself a treat or nourish yourself? Please spend a long time on this section and plan carefully other things to do besides bingeing. You may wish to discuss this with your therapist or a close friend. Develop your own coping responses and write them down here. Refer to this section in the future and add to your list of coping responses:

2. Continue with the binge diary. This time fill out all three columns. If you do binge this week, write down what else you could have done so that you can use that next time you are in a similar situation.

NOTES

WEEKLY BINGE DIARY

NAME _____ WEEK NO. _____

	TIME	WHAT I ATE	FEELINGS AND THOUGHTS PRIOR TO EATING	ALTERNATIVE COPING SKILLS
MONDAY				
TUESDAY				
WEDNESDAY				
THURSDAY				

WEEKLY BINGE DIARY

NAME_____ WEEK NO._____

	TIME	WHAT I ATE	FEELINGS AND THOUGHTS PRIOR TO EATING	ALTERNATIVE COPING SKILLS
F R I D A Y				
S A T U R D A Y				
S U N D A Y				

TOTAL NUMBER OF BINGES THIS WEEK_____

TOTAL NUMBER OF PURGES THIS WEEK_____

WEEK THREE

SELF-ESTEEM, PERFECTIONISM, AND DEPRESSION

If you can't have your piece of the cake, collect all the crumbs you can find.[1]

This chapter is about what to do when you can't have your piece of the cake, when you can't have or be everything you want — in other words, when you are not perfect. Before we discuss how this relates to you, go back and review your binge diary for last week. What do you notice about your binges? Are you using new coping responses? How many binges and purges did you have last week? Has there been a decrease in the number of binges and purges since the previous week? What alternative coping responses have worked for you? What do you still need to work on? Look at the times that you still binged. What happened at those times? Is there a common denominator to your binges? What can you do differently the next time in the same situation? If you are working with your therapist on this, discuss your new coping responses in detail. You need to find techniques that work for you. *Please study your binge diary carefully* and spend a long time on it. Do not just glance at it but examine it thoroughly. If you haven't filled in the third column, go back and do so now. The time you spend now studying your new coping skills and developing new ones can save you a great deal of effort later on. We suggest that you review your binge diary weekly so that you can learn from it and use it to cut down on your binges.

This week we will discuss the relationship between self-esteem, perfectionism and depression and how this relates to you. As we said at the beginning of this book, the research suggests that bulimic women are more perfectionistic, set higher self expectations, have lower self-esteem and are more depressed than other women. How does this apply to you and your eating habits?

Let's talk about perfectionism first. What does it mean to be a perfectionist? And what are its costs and benefits? Perfectionism is not so much the setting of high goals but the setting of *impossible* ones. It's setting your goals so high that nothing you ever do is good enough. This can apply to both personal and weight goals. Let's see how that might apply to you. When is thin enough for you? At what point will you look at yourself and say that this is the right weight for me? Be honest! Most of the women we asked said never. Even those who had a specific weight in mind said that if they reached that goal, they may still not be satisfied. Most women have set their weight goals way below the standards suggested by the Metropolitan Life Insurance Tables.

What about other goals? Do you have a tendency to set your expectations so high that you are defeated before you start? Many perfectionists find out that they cannot attain their goals, and so they become depressed and start feeling bad about themselves since they measure their worth by success and productivity. There appears to be a strong link between perfectionism and depression. When perfectionistic individuals do not attain their goals, they perceive themselves as failures and as inadequate. Their loss of self-esteem can bring about feelings of depression and anxiety.

Are there any advantages to setting extremely high goals? Apparently not, according to the research which suggests that perfectionists do not display better performance because they set high goals.[2] In one study of insurance agents, the perfectionists earned an average of $15,000 a year *less* than the non-perfectionists did. In other studies, athletes with perfectionistic strivings did not perform as well because of their self-doubt and greater difficulty in recovering from mistakes. In school, as well, perfectionists tend to drop out and become depressed because they cannot meet their unrealistic goals.

In addition to feeling depressed and performing more poorly, perfectionists also may be prone to poor health, particularly coronary disease. Perfectionists also are lonely because they are afraid of criticism from others. They are afraid others will not accept them if they are not perfect. The opposite is generally true. Most people are relieved to find that they are "human."

How does all this apply to the binge-purge cycle? Frequently, bulimics will set impossible goals for themselves, both in what they "should" weigh (regardless of what is considered normal for their frames according to the height-weight norms), in how much food they "should" eat, and in how fast they should lose weight. Alice, for example, set her weight goal as 103 pounds (even though her height and frame suggested otherwise). In addition, she set about attaining this unrealistic goal by practically fasting. This was an impossible task as sooner or later her body reacted to the starvation and demanded to be fed. This led to a binge, which resulted in Alice berating herself for not living up to her impossible goal. In addition, she set unrealistic goals for the rate at which she should lose weight. Even though she knew that a weight loss of one or two pounds was about the most she could achieve in a week, she demanded of herself to lose ten pounds in two days, thus getting upset when the scale did not conform to her irrational ideas. Again this led to her feeling depressed, guilty and angry at herself — and eating a whole carton of ice cream to punish herself!

We discussed in the last chapter how our thinking affects the way we behave. Perfectionists generally engage in all-or-nothing thinking which leads them to overreact to mistakes. An extreme example of this is the student who sees anything short of an A+ as a failure. This applies to dieting behavior as well. Mary said she is either on or off a diet. When she's on a diet, she starves. When she's off, she binges. For her, there are no shades of grey. When she eats a small piece of cake after starving herself all day, she says, "Well, I blew it. I'm off my diet now. I might as well eat the whole cake now."

Sarah also applies all-or-nothing thinking to eating. When asked to record her feelings prior to bingeing, she was surprised to learn that she was telling herself, "Well, I'm hungry now. If I just go to the refrigerator, this will lead to a binge!" She learned that she only saw eating in extremes — dieting or bingeing, with no happy medium.

Betty also engaged in all-or-nothing thinking when it came to eating habits. "I either have a good day or a bad day," she said. When questioned what a good day was, she replied that meant she didn't eat anything that day. If she was "bad," meaning she started the day off with a doughnut or something else to put in her mouth, then she may as well continue to be "bad" and gorge herself completely! This all-or-nothing thinking not only led to binges but in her feeling depressed and guilty afterwards, punishing herself for not being able to be "good" all the time, rather than realizing that being "good," i.e., starving, was an impossible goal and doomed to lead to failure.

Betty's behavior is characteristic of the saint-or-sinner syndrome which frequently leads to the failure of the dieting efforts. When perfectionists deviate from the very strict diet goals they set for themselves, the period of sainthood ends and brings in a period of "sin," characterized by guilt, depression and further bingeing. The truth is most of us are not "saints" or "sinners," "good" or "bad," "on" or "off" a diet all the time. Most of us are somewhere in between. Once Mary and Betty could recognize and change their all-or-nothing thinking, they were able to set more realistic goals and

41

not punish themselves so much for not being "good" all the time!

Another kind of thinking that perfectionists engage in is that of overgeneralization. They jump to the conclusion that if one negative instance occurs, it will occur all the time. They generalize from one situation to many. When they make mistakes, they think, "I'm always making mistakes" or "I'll never learn this." Words as "always" or "never" are cues for us that we are generalizing from a specific instance to others. Janet used overgeneralization in her thinking about her bingeing. She had several binges one week, even though she had controlled them in previous weeks. From this, she generalized, "I can't *ever* control my binges." The word "ever" made her aware that she was overreacting to one instance. She learned to change her thinking to "Just because I binged this week doesn't mean I'll never control my binges."

Mary also overgeneralized in her thinking. When she gained some weight, she told herself, "If I gain one pound, I'll gain ten or five." "Why should you gain ten pounds if you gain one?" she was challenged. Mary realized the absurdity of her thinking which only led to feelings of depression. Here are some other examples of overgeneralization:

"I blew it today. I'll always blow it."

"I started the day off wrong. May as well continue bingeing the rest of the day."

"I ate one piece of cake. I can't ever control myself."

Do you ever tell yourself any of the above? In what other situations do you overgeneralize?

Another type of statement that perfectionists make are "should" statements. When perfectionists make mistakes, rather than trying to learn from them, they punish themselves by saying, "I *shouldn't* have done that! I *should* have known better." These "shoulds" make us feel guilty and lead to us feeling that we are not worthwhile. These "shoulds" and "should nots" are extremely harsh and impossible to attain most of the time.

Diane's "shoulds" were very stringent. "I feel I should always be doing something," she said. "If I sit still for one minute, I feel like I am wasting time." "What is doing something?" she was asked. For Diane and for others, "doing something" meant working, studying or engaging in some goal-directed task. Watching television, talking to friends, and even basic bodily functions as sleeping were considered "a waste of time." "I get up at five in the morning," Diane continued, "and I keep going until late at night. Most of the time I don't go to bed until two in the morning, and even then I feel guilty about the time I sleep."

Diane's "shoulds" were so extreme as to be absurd. However, other women related to the feeling that they "should always be doing something." One of the first "shoulds" most of the women cited was "I should study more." No matter how much or how often they studied, they felt it wasn't enough. "How many hours a day should you study?" they were asked. Alice laughed, "At least forty-eight." "When will you feel you have studied enough?" we probed further. "Never," Alice countered, realizing how she set herself up that no matter what she did, she fell short of her standards. In fact, she had defined them as such that there was no way she could ever reach her goal! To add further to her distress, she added, "Even when I do study a lot and feel I have come close to my goal that day, then I get down on myself because I should have been studying this much before. I criticize myself because I haven't done that in the past!" Alice's "shoulds" were so tyrannical that there was no way she could win, no matter what she did.

What are some other "shoulds" women place on themselves? Rhoda, a pleasant, kindhearted woman, said, "I feel I should 'feed the world.' If people are hurting, I feel it is my responsibility to make them feel better. I take on everyone's problems, and I don't say no to anyone, feeling I *should* be able to help everyone. Then I end up feeling tired and drained and resentful, and I feel guilty for feeling that way." Rhoda, like Diane and Alice, has been *extreme* in the demands she made of herself. There was nothing wrong in wanting to help others; however, her "shoulds" demanded that she help *everyone, never* say no, and *"feed the world,"* clearly an impossible task. In addition to feeling guilty for not living up to the impossible image she had of herself, she also felt resentful, which made her feel more guilty, and made it difficult for her to offer help in the manner she wanted to. Rhoda needed to learn to relax her "shoulds" (maybe "feed" one or two people instead of "the world") as well as to "nourish" or "feed" herself first before she could help anyone else. She realized that if she didn't take care of her own needs first, she would be too tired, drained and resentful to be able to give to others.

Dorothy learned to question her "shoulds." "I should get to know everyone in my dorm and be friendly to all of them, but I just haven't really had the time to do that," she said. "Why should you?" she was asked. She looked puzzled, "I don't know, I just should. I never really thought about it." "Do you really want to get to know everyone?" we asked her. "Not particularly," she said. "Then don't do it and don't feel guilty about it," the group told her. Dorothy took a big step by challenging her "shoulds" and focusing instead on "wants." Rather than telling herself "I should do this," she was encouraged to ask herself "Why should I?" and then asking "Do I want to do it?"

Dorothy, like many others, realized that many of the "shoulds" she imposed on herself were arbitrary. When we apply arbitrary rules to ourselves, we tend to rebel against them and not do them, much as a child rebels against an authoritarian parent. Questioning the "shoulds" and changing "I should" statements to "I want" statements can make a big difference in how we perceive and carry out our goals.

Debra and Janet both said "I should be more outgoing." When questioned about their "shoulds," Debra said, "I should be more outgoing because society says it's better to have a lot of friends. I have always been quiet and had one or two close friends. Actually, parties make me nervous, but I feel I should make an effort to be bubbly and gregarious, I guess I don't really want to socialize more. I just feel I should, like it's good for you, like medicine or something." Janet, on the other hand, said this about her desire to be more outgoing: "I would like to be more outgoing because I am missing out on a lot of fun. I would like to learn to relax more around people because my shyness keeps me from making friends, and if I could learn to be more outgoing, I think I would have more fun." Debra is reacting to an arbitrary "should" which she rebels against. She doesn't really want to be more outgoing. She is comfortable with her quietness and having a few close friends but feels she "should" be more outgoing because society thinks that is better than being quiet. She sees it as medicine. Janet, unlike Debra, wants to be more outgoing, not because of some arbitrary standard, but because she wants to have more fun. Janet is probably more likely to carry out her goals than Debra, because Debra does not really wish to and is reacting to some outside, arbitrary standard she does not believe in.

As we asked women what their "shoulds" were, they were surprised to find how unrealistic and impossible were some of the demands they made of themselves. Here are some examples:

"I should"
"be loved by everyone"
"be calling people I don't want to"
"study more — at least 48 hours a day!"
"exercise more"
"practice my music more"
"keep in better contact with all my friends"
"be more responsible"
"be more organized"
"write letters to everyone"
"be able to do it alone"
"be able to do everything and do it well"
"have my room and car clean at all times"

"have tons of energy"
"be more outgoing"
"save my money" (most women made barely enough to pay the rent!)
"do everything right"
"not make mistakes"
"be able to maintain a relationship"
"have someone love me and never look at another woman"
"make everyone happy"
"feed the world"
"be responsible for other peoples' happiness"
"be more skinny"
"stop bingeing completely"
"sleep less"

Study those "shoulds." Do you relate to any of them? Write your own list of "should" statements:

"I should"

Go back to your list. Which of these are realistic? Which are not? Put a *U* by those that are unrealistic. Now review the list again and ask yourself *why* you "should" be or do each of these things. Is it an arbitrary "should" or is it an "I want?" Write *A* or **arbitrary** for those "shoulds" that you really are not doing for yourself but because of what you think society, your parents or another authority demands from you. For those statements that are both realistic and wants, try to go back and lower your expectations. Statements such as

45

"I should study more" or "practice more" or "clean my room more" leave us feeling guilty because no matter what we do, it is never enough. We should always be doing more. Change those statements to manageable goals. For example, rather than saying, "I should practice more," change that to "I want to practice two hours a week." If your goal is to be more organized, change that to "I would like to clean my desk within the next two weeks."

Go back over the statements you have. Cross out the ones that are completely impossible and unrealistic. Also cross out the ones that are arbitrary "shoulds" rather than "wants." Now make a new list of "I wants" and define the goals more concretely.

"I want"

How does it feel to change the "shoulds" to "wants?" Are you more likely to carry them out?

We have asked you to lower your expectations so that you can meet your goals more readily and have a feeling of accomplishment. Many perfectionists assume that setting the highest possible standards will result in an optimal performance and satisfaction. They feel that if they set extremely high goals, they can then motivate themselves to do their best. You may feel some anxiety about having to lower your expectations. "Why should I aim for anything but the best?" you might ask yourself. The truth is that you cannot be "the best" at all times. Anything you do will be below your own average half the time and above your average the other half. It is statistically impossible to do your best all the time since by defini-

46

tion the "best" can only happen once. If you aim for more modest accomplishments, the chances that you will accomplish those and even go beyond them are high. As one woman we know likes to say, "I don't need to be perfect. My mediocre is good enough."

"What else can I do about my perfectionism besides lowering my standards?" is a question that is frequently asked. Let us get back to Rhoda who so much wanted to "feed the world" that she was drained and tired all the time. Much as she wanted to help everyone, she found that she had neither the time nor the energy to give as much as she wanted. Rhoda was so busy "feeding" everyone else, she was not taking care of herself. She put everybody else's needs ahead of her own.

"But isn't it selfish to think of yourself first?" she asked. "Everyone teaches you to put others first." Rhoda expressed what many people think when they are asked to put their needs first. They think "selfish" is a dirty word. The truth is that selfish means loving yourself and taking care of yourself. And it is the people who are good to themselves who are most able to give to others. If we are good to ourselves and nourish ourselves with rest and gentleness, then we have the resources and energy to give to others. If we are tired, on the other hand, or cross and nervous because we have not had a moment to ourselves all day, we are very unlikely to be of much use to anyone. We owe it to ourselves and to others to "nourish" ourselves in little ways.

Take a few minutes to ask yourself "How can I 'nourish' myself besides bingeing?" "In what other ways can I give myself a 'treat' besides food?" Donna said she loved to go out and buy some lingerie for herself. Others agreed that buying gifts and clothes for themselves was a real "treat." Many women felt too guilty to do that. It was okay for them to buy gifts for others, but they felt guilty and "selfish" for spending the money on themselves. "I like to take a long bubble bath and listen to some good music. That really makes me feel luxurious, but it's a treat I don't give myself too often because I feel I should be doing something else," said Connie. Again, she expressed guilt that she was "wasting" time on something so unimportant (herself!) and her overcritical "shoulds" got in the way of giving herself pleasure.

Other ways of nourishing ourselves are by watching television, reading the Sunday paper from cover to cover, sleeping in, going to a show, meditating, taking a nap, buying sweet-smelling soap and perfume and other little treats that give us the feeling of being pampered and cared for.

Talking to ourselves nicely is another way of nourishing ourselves. "I tell myself, 'you did a good job'" or "you're doing the best you can," said Rita. "I'm really trying hard to talk nicely and kindly to myself, the way I would talk to someone else. I realize how critical I have been of me." "I count my blessings and tell myself how lucky I am to have what I have, instead of all the things I'm doing wrong. That always soothes me," said another woman. Other women were also learning to whisper kind, gently encouraging statements to themselves, to "nourish" themselves with positive thoughts rather than with food.

Friends also serve as "nourishers." Calling friends on the telephone or going out with people who care about you are good ways of nourishing ourselves. Good friends are those who support and encourage us and can serve as a real "treat." Rhoda said that being hugged was another way of giving herself a treat. "Also, if I'm really feeling low, I call my friends and ask them to say some nice things about me. This really helps me feel good about myself again." Other women said that laughing with friends and doing "goofy" things together were also treats they gave themselves from time to time. Some relationships are more nourishing than others. Think of the friends you have that nourish you. With whom do you feel most comfortable? Which of those people do you wish to spend more time with?

Ask yourself "how can I nourish myself?" as you fill out the following:

How Can I Nourish Myself?

1. What situations makes me feel good? (Make sure you put "fun" things here, not goal-oriented activities as "being prepared for class," etc.)

2. Which relationships are nourishing? Why?

3. What do I *say* and *do* to make myself feel good? Make a list and keep adding to it.

Many women did not allow themselves many of the "treats" because they felt they did not deserve them. If you feel that you do not deserve those treats, we would like you to start appreciating yourself more and liking yourself better. We'd like you to start out by making a list of your positive qualities, things you like about yourself. Even if you cannot think of anything you particularly like about yourself at this moment because you are feeling low or for some other reason, write down what you have appreciated about yourself at other times in the past. When we feel depressed, we may forget some of our good qualities. Also write down what others have said they like about you. The positive quality does not need to be "perfect" before you can put it down. For example, if you have been told that you are pretty, put that down, even if you are tempted to add, "Yes, but my nose is too long." Or if you are generally organized, put that down even if you are forgetful at times. Write at least ten qualities now and keep adding to the list until you can reach 30.

MY POSITIVE QUALITIES

1.
2.
3.
4.
5.
6.
7.
8.
9.
10.
11.
12.
13.
14.
15.
16.
17.
18.
19.
20.
21.
22.
23.
24.
25.
26.
27.
28.
29.
30.

HOMEWORK

1. Add to your "I should," nourishing activities and positive qualities lists.

2. Pick one thing from your list of nourishing activities and do it.

3. Ask three people (one who knows you at work or school, one family member and one friend) to tell you what they like about you and record below. We are aware that this may be difficult to do but do it anyway. You may tell them that you are doing this as part of your homework for a class, if you wish to make it easier for yourself to ask them.

What Others Like About Me

Coworker or Classmate

Family Member

Friend

4. Continue your binge diary.

51

NOTES

WEEKLY BINGE DIARY

NAME_____ WEEK NO._____

	TIME	WHAT I ATE	FEELINGS AND THOUGHTS PRIOR TO EATING	ALTERNATIVE COPING SKILLS
MONDAY				
TUESDAY				
WEDNESDAY				
THURSDAY				

WEEKLY BINGE DIARY

NAME_____ WEEK NO._____

	TIME	WHAT I ATE	FEELINGS AND THOUGHTS PRIOR TO EATING	ALTERNATIVE COPING SKILLS
F R I D A Y				
S A T U R D A Y				
S U N D A Y				

TOTAL NUMBER OF BINGES THIS WEEK_____

TOTAL NUMBER OF PURGES THIS WEEK_____

WEEK FOUR

ANGER AND ASSERTIVENESS

"I swallow my anger and then I throw it up." —
A bulimic woman.

Our language is filled with expressions relating anger to eating behavior. How many times do we "swallow" our emotions? How often do we feel that we just "can't digest" or are "fed up" with something? How often do we state that we "have had it up to here," as we point to our throats? How many people or situations make us "want to puke?" In how many situations do we "eat our words?" As we stated at the beginning of this book, research findings indicate that bulimics have more difficulty than non-bulimics expressing emotional negative states such as anger. If you are "eating" your anger or letting it "eat at you" at times, you will find this chapter very helpful.

The focus of this chapter is to help you express your feelings in an open, direct manner — in short, assertively. What is assertiveness? What does it mean to express ourselves assertively? Assertiveness is stating our feelings openly and directly without hurting ourselves or hurting anyone else. Frequently, it is confused with aggression which is also open expression of feelings but this is usually done at the expense of someone else. Non-assertive behavior is when we don't express our feelings and let others step all over us. It means our rights are easily violated.

As you study these terms, you might find out that at different times and with different people, you may have behaved in either one of the three styles of behavior. For example, Alice said she alternated between behaving like a "doormat" and a "bitch" with her boyfriend. "I am real sweet to him and tell him whatever I think he wants to hear. Then we end up doing what he wants all the time; so I get real angry and blow up at him. For example, he'll ask me if I want to go to Burger King or Pizza Hut, and I'll say Burger King because I think that's what he wants whereas I'd really like to go to Pizza Hut. Then I get resentful and act like a bitch the rest of the evening." Alice's behavior is typical of others who do not express themselves directly. They don't say what they feel in an attempt to be "nice." Then they get angry afterwards. Alice would have avoided much of her problem by just speaking up in the first place.

Other women expressed that they could be quite assertive with some people but not with others. "I can tell people anything that's on my mind at work but I just can't seem to stand up to my husband," said Dina. Others could identify with her. The truth is that nobody is totally assertive or totally unassertive. Most of us are more assertive in some situations and with some people than with others.

As you study the definition of assertion, you may notice the word "rights" appears. Assertion is standing up for our rights. Many of us may not express ourselves assertively because we are not aware of what our rights are. Spend a few minutes writing down your rights.

My Basic Human Rights

Let's study some of the human rights we have. These include, among others, the right to express ourselves as long as we don't hurt others, to refuse a request without feeling guilty, to express anger and to judge for ourselves.[2]

One of the rights that many women do not exercise is that of saying no without feeling guilty about it. Rhoda, for example, who wanted to "feed the world," felt she could not say no to anyone who asked for help. She was involved in too many activities and was finding it impossible to keep up with her schoolwork and meet her own needs. She was feeling run-down, tired and depressed. "Which of these activities can you give up?" she was asked. "I can't give up any of these," she said. "Everyone is counting on me. Yet I can't give up my schoolwork or my friends. I want to do everything." Like many others, Rhoda's feeling that she should be able to do everything was self-defeating. "There is only one thing you need to give up," she was told, "and that is your image of yourself as being perfect." Once Rhoda was able to accept that she does not need to be perfect and does not need to do everything well, she could give up some of her extracurricular activities.

Living up to an image is a big reason why so many women say yes when they really want to say no to requests. "I'm afraid people will think I'm not capable if I say I can't do something. So I take on everything. I want people to say, 'Look at her. She can handle anything',"" said Marilyn, an attractive, capable woman who had a tremendous need to be liked. Others could identify with her. "I guess I want to prove I can do it all," said Alice, "so I just go from one thing to another until I'm exhausted. The crazy thing is I *volunteer* for things at times without anyone even asking me to do something." Saying no to others or even to themselves is very hard for many people.

If you are saying yes only to end up feeling exploited and resentful, you are probably saying yes for the wrong reasons. Some of the most common reasons for saying yes are to win approval and acceptance and to avoid hurting someone's feelings. We are afraid that if we refuse someone's requests, they will stop liking us. The truth is that some people are not going to like us regardless of what we do, and in fact, sometimes too much niceness can make others uncomfortable. We don't need everyone's approval, but if we assert ourselves, we may get their respect, and that is more important.

Another wrong reason for saying yes when you want to say no is to convince yourself that you are a good person. You may be saying yes to make up for imagined or real failures. For example, many working mothers feel guilty for leaving their child and then try to make up for it by overindulging him. If you are constantly saying yes when you would really like to say no, remind yourself that you have a *right* to say no. In fact, you deny your own importance when you say yes when you don't want to. You are not rejecting another person when you say no — only the request. Try saying no directly, without going into long explanations, and don't apologize for refusing. You will find that saying no and not feeling guilty about it can become a habit that will decrease your stress.

Besides saying no to requests, assertive behavior is also expressing anger directly rather than "stuffing it in" or "spitting it out." Think of a specific situation when you were angry and did not express anger the way you wanted. Ask yourself the following questions and record your answers.

1. To whom was my anger directed?

2. What did I actually do or say?

3. What did I want to do or say?

4. What were my fears behind saying or doing what I wanted to?

"I had made plans to go out with this guy and he was over half an hour late. I was really angry since I was out waiting in the cold, and besides, we were late for the movies, and I thought it was really inconsiderate of him, but I pretended it was okay. I was afraid if I told him how I felt, he'd get angry too and would not ask me out again."

"I was at work minding my own business when this man gave me a tongue-lashing I didn't deserve. I wanted to tell him I didn't deserve to be spoken to like that, but I was afraid if I spoke up, I'd start to cry, so I kept my mouth shut and went back home and cried my eyes out."

"My mother was putting me down as usual about not living up to her expectations. I was furious but I didn't say anything because I was afraid of what I'd say. I was afraid if I really expressed myself, I would blow up and then regret it afterwards. Or she would stop loving me. So I just kept it inside and stuffed it until I got an ulcer."

Fears of their reaction or other people's reactions to anger were what kept many women from expressing themselves. They were afraid they would either lose control and look foolish by crying or by striking out and doing or saying something they would regret later. They were also afraid of reprisal if they got angry — afraid that the other person would strike back or would stop caring for them. For some women, anger was so threatening that they could not recall a single instance when they felt angry.

We had to assure those women that anger is a normal, healthy emotion. Anger and violence are not synonymous, as many people believe. Expressing anger can be done quietly, politely, and tact-fully — in other words, assertively. Sometimes the most appropriate angry response is to leave a room or in other ways indicate that you are angered by the message. In other situations, you may deliberately choose not to express anger if the consequences can indeed be harm-ful, as when one is holding a gun on you. However, in most situa-tions, anger *if expressed assertively*, can be very constructive.

In some situations, we may choose to control our anger. We need to control our inner rage so that we can speak politely and assertively instead of striking out. In those situations, the messages we tell ourselves can help calm us down so that we can express ourselves confidently. We have discussed before how talking to our-selves and changing the way we think can influence our behavior. This holds true for anger situations as well. Think, for example, of a situation where someone is being deliberately nasty. If you tell yourself, "That bastard! I won't let him get away with this!" you are likely to get more enraged. If instead you tell yourself, "I'll just let him make a fool of himself," you do not need to get so upset by his provocation. Think of other things you can tell yourself to calm you down when you are feeling enraged. Sometimes count-ing to ten and telling yourself to relax can help you express your anger in a calm manner.

Once you are able to calm yourself down, the next step is to express your anger. The best way to express anger is to use "I" statements. "I feel angry right now" is less likely to alienate someone than "you" messages as "you make me so mad." Express why you are feeling angry without labeling the person and make a direct request for change. For example, "I'm angry that you didn't do the dishes as you promised. I'd appreciate your doing them in the future" is more likely to get a positive response and not elicit hard feelings than "You're a no-good slob. You re irresponsible and never keep your promise." Practice expressing your anger in an assertive man-ner. If you express it as it happens and don't let it build up, you will not "stuff" it to a point where you will want to "spit it up." If you are working with a therapist, you may want to rehearse some of your assertiveness skills by role-playing some difficult situations.

HOMEWORK

1. Review the material on assertiveness, basic human rights, saying no and expressing your anger.

2. This exercise is adapted from Lonnie Barbach and called the

Yes's and No's.3

Say no to three things that you didn't want to do anyway but feel you *should* do. This could be to someone else or to yourself. For example, you can say no to babysitting for your niece when you don't feel like it or you can say no to going out with someone you don't like when you don't feel like it. You can also say no to doing the laundry or cleaning up your closet when you feel like doing something else. Say yes to three things that you really want but would not usually let yourself have or ask others for. You can buy that new dress or new book that you wanted but didn't feel you could let yourself have or you can go ahead and sleep an extra hour or take that luxurious bath you don't have time for. Or you can let your friends do something nice for you. Go ahead, say yes! Record these:

NO'S

1.

2.

3.

YES'S

1.

2.

3.

3. Note situations this week in which you felt angry and how you handled them. Record these. How did you feel you handled them? What changes do you need to make?

Situations that made me angry   **How I handled them**

4. Continue your binge diary.

NOTES

WEEKLY BINGE DIARY

NAME_____ WEEK NO._____

	TIME	WHAT I ATE	FEELINGS AND THOUGHTS PRIOR TO EATING	ALTERNATIVE COPING SKILLS
MONDAY				
TUESDAY				
WEDNESDAY				
THURSDAY				

WEEKLY BINGE DIARY

NAME_____ WEEK NO._____

	TIME	WHAT I ATE	FEELINGS AND THOUGHTS PRIOR TO EATING	ALTERNATIVE COPING SKILLS
F R I D A Y				
S A T U R D A Y				
S U N D A Y				

TOTAL NUMBER OF BINGES THIS WEEK_____

TOTAL NUMBER OF PURGES THIS WEEK_____

CULTURAL EXPECTATIONS OF THINNESS FOR WOMEN

You can never be too rich or too thin.

This remark, reportedly made by the Duchess of Windsor, summarizes succinctly the societal expectations of thinness for women. In order to be a "real" woman, one has to be thin. If a woman is slim, then she will be loved and accepted by men. Susie Orbach discusses at length the societal pressures on women to be thin.[1] She states that our society emphasizes presentation as a central aspect of a woman's existence. This makes the woman very self-conscious as she scrutinizes and judges herself in an effort to make herself in the image presented by the media so that she can "catch" a man. In order to live up to this image, she becomes prey to the diet and fashion industry that tries to remold her body to conform to the ideal physical type. The woman's body is not all right the way it is and has to constantly be remodeled, deodorized, perfumed and free of excess hair. This job of remodeling and refashioning women's bodies is never-ending for the image changes on a yearly basis. Women's bodies are expected to change seasonally, just as styles in clothes change. The voluptuous, large breasted woman is "in" one year, the twiggy type the next. Although the image of the perfect woman may change from year to year, one factor remains constant: that a woman remain slim.

To be thin is thus to be the ideal woman. What is the ideal woman? Does such a creature exist? Take a few minutes to visualize the perfect woman to yourself. What is she like? What does she look like?

"The perfect woman is tall and thin," said Rhoda. "Above all, she must have long legs, together with a flat abdomen and rear end."

"The perfect woman must also be healthy looking," added Alice. "It's important nowadays to look healthy and have some

61

muscles. She needs to have a good tan."

"And white, bright, even teeth," Carla chimed in.

"Her skin must be flawless. No wrinkles, pimples or blemishes," said another woman.

"She must look young," added the others. "Once she's over a certain age, she's over the hill." Although there was some disagreement as to at what age one stopped being perfect, clearly once a woman was in her thirties – or, heaven forbid, forties or more – she was no longer the ideal woman.

"The ideal woman has smooth legs. No hair on her arms or legs or under her arms. She must not be just well shaved. She just doesn't have hair on her legs! You don't see any models whose legs look like they once had hair on them," Diana said.

"The perfect woman has perfect features: a straight nose, beautiful eyes and mouth. Her hair is long and shiny," added Carla. "She is always immaculately groomed, not a hair out of place. Her makeup never smears, and she wears the latest styles. She looks wonderful at all times, morning, noon and night. You never see her in curlers or without makeup. Her nails are always manicured and have nail polish on them."

"One other criterion," said Rhoda. "She must do all this effortlessly. She just 'naturally' looks great all the time, without any work or effort."

"Doing it effortlessly" apparently extended to other areas. "She should be bright, career-oriented, successful at work, at the same time that she takes care of a house, husband and kids," said Diana. "She should be very successful in her career as well as a gourmet cook."

This sentiment was echoed by others. The perfect woman should do "everything well" and do it "effortlessly." She should have endless energy and do everything thoroughly, efficiently and without any effort. Does such a woman exist? Only in television commercials where a woman changes within seconds from the successful executive to the gourmet cook to the sexpot at night. Yet women all over are trying hard to live up to this unrealistic image of Superwoman and feeling depressed and disappointed because they are human.

What are the payoffs of trying to be the perfect woman? What benefits do we gain when we come close to this Superwoman image? "When I am really slim and feel I'm looking my best, it gives me a feeling of confidence. I feel I can lick the world. I feel 'gorgeous'," said Rhoda. Others echoed the feeling: "It feels good to be slim." "I feel I'm attractive and sexy." "I feel good knowing I look good." Certainly confidence and feeling good about our looks are important.

Other advantages include attention from men. "When I really

feel I look my best, then I get a lot of male attention. I get compliments from others, and that makes me feel good," said Alice.

"I don't know if it's because I look better or because I feel better about myself, but I get a great deal of attention from men. I feel more accepted by them," said Carla.

"I guess it makes me feel good to look slim so others can say, 'Isn't she wonderful. She looks so good and she also is successful.' I guess even though I know I'm not Superwoman, I want others to think I am," said Diana.

Confidence, attention from men, admiration from others. . . these are certainly things to aim for, aren't they? Do they make the excessive dieting worthwhile? What is the price we pay in our efforts to be the "perfect woman"? How do we abuse ourselves and our bodies to achieve this goal?

"When I think of what I'm doing to my body just so I can fit into a certain size, I shudder," Diana reported. "It really scares me when I realize all the physical problems I can have and what I'm doing to my health."

"I feel starved and deprived all the time," said another woman. "I am tired and irritable. That's a big price to pay for a few seconds of male attention."

"Besides," said Alice, "all this attention is only temporary. So is the feeling of security. If he only loves me when I look my best, then I'll always worry about what will happen if he sees me without makeup or not looking my best."

Rhoda agreed with that. "Thinness does not give you a sense of security. It makes me feel insecure if I feel that people only like me for my looks. I know I'll be older one day, and I don't want to get depressed just because I have a few wrinkles and gray hair."

Doris could relate to this feeling of insecurity. "I guess no matter how thin I am or how good people tell me I look, I always feel it's not good enough. I always strive harder to look better and get thinner and I get depressed because I'll never look like the perfect woman."

"I feel like a failure when I don't look and act like the perfect woman. I always fall short of that regardless of what I do; so I constantly feel depressed because I don't look like the magazines say I should," another woman said.

It appears that contrary to the belief that we will feel secure and happy if we look like the perfect woman, the truth is that trying to achieve an impossible ideal only leads to further insecurity and unhappiness. The security is superficial and only based on surface appearances.

The amount of time and effort required to be slim is another price we pay in our obsession to look like the "perfect woman."

Contrary to the myth that models look gorgeous "effortlessly," in fact it takes a great deal of time, discipline and hard work to look like they do. Models spend an inordinate amount of time in looking immaculate. We have to realize, however, that this is their *job*. They are getting paid to look and dress in a certain way, and they work at this job just as we work at ours. For most of us, immaculate grooming is not essential to our careers, and the hard work and effort is simply not worth it unless we want to make that an all-consuming part of our life. Carmela, a secretary, made this observation: "I realized suddenly that many of these models are getting paid thousands of dollars to look a certain way. It's their career and so they go to extreme lengths to look good. I don't need to do that. I sit behind a desk most of the time, and most people only see my face. It's ridiculous to spend so much energy trying to lose a few pounds when it really makes no difference for me. If I were getting paid to lose those pounds, it would be a different matter. I have to remind myself that for models it's a career to be slim, and that my career is as a secretary."

This is not to suggest that looking "good" is not important. It is the *excessive* attention paid to dieting at the cost of everything else that limits us and for which we pay a heavy price. The time and effort in thinking, planning, and worrying about that extra pound could be spent in more important ways. "You know," Alice said, "I realized how really *boring* it is to just talk about my weight. I mean, there are so many other things to talk about and so many other aspects of me that I could develop. I spend all my time and energy on that pound or two instead of the other things I could do."

"I miss out on having fun," said Alice. "I don't go out to eat which I'd really enjoy because I'm afraid I'll gain weight. I don't laugh as much or say what I feel because I might not be like the super-cool, perfect woman. I miss out on friends because I don't dare really be myself with them."

"I think the biggest price we pay for trying to adhere to this notion of the 'perfect woman' is that we lose ourselves and our identity." said Rhoda. "I'm trying so hard to be what I think society demands that I am no longer being myself. I don't meet my own needs."

Health, emotions, fun, time, effort, friendship, our identity — these are the costs of trying to be the ideal woman. Is being slim worth the heavy price we pay? For most women, this was an eye-opener. "I realize how lopsided and distorted my values are," said Rita. "I mean, it's good to be slim but, my God, there are more important things. Besides, I can be slim but it doesn't have to take up my whole life!"

Other women also became aware of how their efforts to be the "perfect woman" extended to their relationships with men. How is the perfect woman supposed to be around men? All of the women agreed that the ideal woman was "feminine" in her interactions with men. This applied both to her looks ("tiny, demure, pretty, dainty") as well as to her actions. In addition to always looking "perfect,"a truly "feminine" woman was deferential to men. She was attuned to their needs and generally dependent on them. She was a follower rather than a leader and waited for men to take the initiative. She was a giver, caring and never getting angry. A truly feminine woman was also "weak" and needed a man to put up with her "emotionality."

Although many women intellectually rejected this stereotype of "feminine" behavior and felt it didn't apply to them, they were surprised to find that in their behavior, they related differently to men than they did to women. If you would like to explore your relationships with men, stop for a few minutes and think to yourself of how you act when you are alone with other women and how you act when you are around attractive men. Record your reactions.

How I Act With Women   **How I Act With Men**

"I'm more conscious of the way I look and act when I'm around men, particularly those I find attractive," said Rhoda. "I'm just more self-conscious and not as comfortable with them."

This sentiment was expressed over and over by women. The self-consciousness expressed itself in women "performing" more for men, whether by being witty and charming or by becoming shy and tongue-tied. "If I'm with a man I find the least bit attractive, I become uncomfortable. I blush, stutter and generally find it hard to articulate my thoughts. I may even giggle, which really bothers me. With women, I can be more relaxed and comfortable. I can be myself and don't feel so self-conscious," said another woman.

"I'm more stilted and awkward when I'm with a man than a woman. It's as though I can't really relax and be myself. I'm always self-conscious, always aware that he's watching me," said another woman.

"I'm more coy with men," added another woman. "I play the typical roles, acting helpless, doing what I think men like, saying yes to what I think they want, doing things to get their approval."

"I'm wittier around men than when I'm around women. Sometimes I'm more caustic or sarcastic. I tease more and joke more," said Alice. "I guess again I am performing for them."

"I'm more defensive with men about their motives and desires. I trust women more and can be more open and honest with them than I can with men," added Carla. "With men, I play games."

Other women also felt less trusting and open with men. At those times when they felt they didn't trust other women, it was usually when they were competing for a man's approval. Women also tended to see men as more important than women. "You can be with a group of women engaged in a conversation and the second a man shows up, all the attention is focused on him. We interrupt our conversation and turn to him," said Joanne.

"It's like it's okay to cancel plans you made with a woman just because you get asked on a date with a man. It's as though saying men come first," said Rhoda.

"With women I can express myself. If I want a sweet, I can say I want a sweet. If a man is there, I don't say what I want. His needs come first. I'm embarrased to say what I want," Carol said.

"If we go to a restaurant, I will eat less when I'm with a man so he'll think I'm 'feminine.' When I'm with a woman, I eat whatever I like," added Alice.

In all these statements, women were viewing men as evaluators and themselves as products to be evaluated. They were self-conscious around men, "performed" for them and sought their approval. They put men's needs ahead of their own in their relationships and in their behavior acted as though men were more important than women. With women, they could be themselves. They felt more comfortable, relaxed and accepted.

In women's efforts to be products that would be evaluated positively by men, they subjected themselves to the stringent dieting and abuses to their bodies. In addition, in their attempts to "catch" a man, they tended to deny their needs and self-importance.

If you can identify within yourself some of the ways in which you behave differently when you are around men than when you are around women, you may wish to change some of your behavior. If you're serious about change, go back to your list and mark which of the behaviors you display around men are advantageous for you and which are not. Which ones do you want to keep? Which would you like to get rid of?

Awareness is a major key to action. By becoming aware of your behavior around men, you then have a choice of which behaviors you want to keep and which ones you don't. Begin practicing new behaviors, perhaps one at a time and see if you find this behavior more effective. See if you bring about changes in the way men relate to you too.

You might experiment with little steps, for example, not trying to be "witty" and "perform" for an attractive man. Is there a difference in the way you feel? In the way he relates to you? Or if you find yourself breaking a date with a close girlfriend when "he" calls because he is special and she's your best friend and she'll understand, tell him you have made plans with your girlfriend already. Or the next time you are with a man and you want to order something you like or go to a movie you want, say so. Notice what happens to you when you express your needs, even if it's not what he wants.

Awareness of how much we are conditioned to be products for men to evaluate and how impossible it is to live up to the impossible goal of being the "perfect woman" also means we can start accepting and loving our bodies, with "unwanted" hair, pimples, wrinkles and all, even if it doesn't adhere to what is "in" for bodies this year.

When was the last time you looked at your body? It is time now to start becoming friends with it.

HOMEWORK

1. This week we will ask you to do a few exercises to make you more comfortable with your body. The first exercise is adapted from Lonnie Barbach's Body Mirror Exercise.[2] Take an hour when you can be uninterrupted and insured of privacy. Set up

a full-length mirror in the privacy of your room or bathroom. If you don't have one, go out and buy one! Get into a relaxed mood. How you choose to do this will vary. You might take a nice bubble bath, drink a glass of wine, listen to music, or all of these. Now stand undressed in front of the mirror and study your body from all sides and angles. Carefully examine your body, talking to yourself as you are looking, telling yourself what you like. Start from your hair and go down to your toes. For example, Diana said, "I like my hair. It is thick and brown and curly. It's smooth and soft. I like my smile. I love my long neck. I love my firm breasts. . . ." going through each and every body part. Most women found to their surprise that what they appreciated most about their bodies wasn't just physical appearance but the function a part served. For example, Rhoda said she enjoyed her athletic abilities. Diana, although she had tiny ears, had an excellent sense of hearing which was very useful to her.

Look at yourself for at least fifteen or twenty minutes. Study your facial features and your body from all angles. You may have some difficulty carrying out this exercise because you may be expecting the worst. If you are like most of the others, you have probably not looked at your body for such a long time that you may have exaggerated its negative aspects in your mind. Look at your body until you learn to like it. If there are some parts you don't care for, such as a protruding stomach or "love handles," exaggerate those by sticking them out until you are comfortable with them. *This is your body. Learn to love it and become friends with it because it will be with you for the rest of your life.*

After you have looked at yourself thoroughly for fifteen or twenty minutes, start exploring your body with your hands. Again, talk to yourself about what your hands are feeling. Run your fingers over your body and feel the varied textures of your skin. Maybe you can discover something you didn't know before. Learn to understand and like your body.

Record what you like about your body. Keep adding to your list.

What I Like About My Body

2. Ask three men to tell you which women they consider sexy and why. Ask them to pick women you know or to point to someone (movie stars and models excluded). Record your reactions. Are you surprised by what you hear? This exercise is designed to help you become aware of what others consider sexy or attractive. Many women are surprised to discover that fairly average-looking women who do not fit the "perfect" woman image are considered sexy or attractive by men. They are also surprised to find out that other factors than weight are mentioned in defining a person's attractiveness.

Who is sexy and attractive   **Why**   **My reactions**

3. Find a magazine photo of someone whose body you think looks like yours and one of someone whose body you wish to look like. Paste these photos on the next page. Ask your friends for feedback. Most women saw themselves as much chunkier than others saw them. They had a distorted picture of their body and saw it more negatively. Ask your friends for a more realistic picture of yourself. Learn to see yourself more realistically.

4. Continue your binge diary.

A photo of what I wish to look like

A photo of how I think I look

Feedback from my friends

NOTES

WEEKLY BINGE DIARY

NAME_____ WEEK NO._____

	TIME	WHAT I ATE	FEELINGS AND THOUGHTS PRIOR TO EATING	ALTERNATIVE COPING SKILLS
MONDAY				
TUESDAY				
WEDNESDAY				
THURSDAY				

WEEKLY BINGE DIARY

NAME_____ WEEK NO._____

	TIME	WHAT I ATE	FEELINGS AND THOUGHTS PRIOR TO EATING	ALTERNATIVE COPING SKILLS
F R I D A Y				
S A T U R D A Y				
S U N D A Y				

TOTAL NUMBER OF BINGES THIS WEEK_____

TOTAL NUMBER OF PURGES THIS WEEK_____

ENHANCING BODY IMAGE

My body is falling so fast my gynecologist wears a hard hat. — Joan Rivers, Comedienne

Beneath the humor and jokes we make about our bodies there is a great deal of underlying pain. For most women, their feelings about their bodies tend to be a source of anxiety and hurt, regardless of their physical appearance. The depth of this hurt was dramatically illustrated in a women's weekend workshop that took place over ten years ago. Women of all ages and body types attended this workshop in a comfortable, intimate setting where mutual trust and friendship were established. Toward the end of the workshop, women divided into small groups and discussed their feelings about their bodies. There was a strikingly attractive woman at the workshop. She had "perfect" features and a tall, slender body appearing as though she had just stepped out of the magazine pages. She looked, by anyone's standards, like the prototype of today's female fashion models. Although we were not surprised to hear other women with more "imperfect" features express pain and concern about their bodies, we were totally unprepared for the intense reaction of this unusually beautiful woman. She sobbed uncontrollably as she talked about her small breasts and how "ugly" she felt because she didn't have a good body. For her, the "perfect woman" was "stacked" and "curvy." She also was too "tall" and therefore not "feminine." This workshop took place over ten years ago when big breasts were "in." This woman spent her adolescence looking at magazines which featured Jayne Mansfield, Marilyn Monroe and other sex symbols whose attractiveness was measured by the size of their bra cups. Had she been born twenty years later, her body may have been more in line with the 1980's small-chested, tall model-types.

Ironically, many young women today who have large breasts

73

and well-rounded curves are experiencing the same hurt and frustrations because their bodies don't correspond to today's willowy model types. Doris is one such example. Doris is a very attractive woman with big brown eyes, attractive tan and flowing long hair. Others would describe her as "stacked," and she has the well-rounded bosom that would have been the source of envy by the woman at the workshop a decade earlier. Doris, however, feels her body is ugly and cries as she talks about it.

Designers of women's clothing, magazines and movies set different standards of what a woman should look like each year. If a woman is not this year's model, she feels like a failure. A body can be "in" one year and "out" the next, and to try to rearrange the body to fit the times is ridiculous. However, many women have considerable anguish and try to go against the natural contours of their bodies. Even if there is agreement as to what is beautiful in bodies, the truth is that most women will not look like Raquel Welch, Jane Fonda or any number of other beauties regardless of what they do. They could spare themselves much anguish if they accepted what they looked like instead of having a negative body image. In addition, our society does not allow for those body changes that normally take place as we grow older. Many women unfortunately torture themselves *simply because their bodies are doing what they are supposed to.*

Alice is a good example of someone who is trying to go against her own natural body contours. "I look at the women in my family," she said, "and we all have large, well-rounded breasts and big thighs. We are not fat, just curvy. Yet I keep trying to look like a beanpole. I know that no matter what I do I won't look like a skinny model simply because this is my *body shape* — I wonder why I'm trying to change nature."

"In addition," she added, "I keep trying to get rid of my rounded stomach." We asked Alice what she feels her stomach should look like, and she promptly responded, "Concave." Then she laughed, "I know in reality that women's tummies are not concave and that it is not anatomically possible but I still want mine to be sucked in."

Alice had a further insight in other ways in which she was trying to go against the nature of her body. "I just realized," she said, "that years ago I used to look like a beanpole. I was straight all over, I had practically no breasts, no hips, no curves. I am still trying to look like I did then *but years ago I was a child!* My body is now a woman's body but I'm still trying to make it look like it did when I was thirteen."

Despite Alice's awareness that she was trying to artificially fit her body into a mold, she still felt depressed over her perceived imperfections. Alice, like many other women with a negative body image, let her feelings about her body interfere with her deriving pleasure from it. "I love to be stroked and caressed," she said, "particularly on my tummy. But I don't let my boyfriend stroke me there or even look at me without clothes on because I feel so fat." Alice, in fact, had a very attractive figure, and her "rounded" tummy would be considered flat by most people. "My boyfriend thinks I look beautiful. He loves my body. He tells me he likes to touch flesh, not skin and bones, but I just can't seem to relax sexually."

Alice, like many other women who didn't like their bodies, found that this interfered with her sexual enjoyment. She could not let herself relax so that she would derive the sexual satisfaction and intimacy she wanted even though she recognized the absurdity of her actions. "I know the last thing he is thinking of when we are making love is the size of my waistline. He can't even see me in the dark. Yet I am so self-conscious about it." Our culture places such a value on physical attractiveness that some women inhibit themselves from having an orgasm for fear that they will look ugly while they are doing so and repulse their partners.

The situation is even more difficult for women who are in fact rather heavy and whose partners, unlike Alice's boyfriend, are not supportive. Connie's husband was constantly nagging at her to lose weight and telling her that she was too fat. Furthermore, he frequently rejected her sexually, which only increased her negative feelings about her body. Connie soothed her feelings of anger and rejection by turning to food to comfort her.

The negative feelings about their bodies and lack of sexual satisfaction lead many women to binge, substituting food for sex and love. Unfortunately, the bingeing only leads to further negative feelings about the body, which leads to more bingeing, and a vicious cycle can ensue. Many women reported that they used bingeing as a substitute for sexual satisfaction and intimacy. Connie, who generally binged after a sexual rejection from her husband, learned to meet her sexual needs more directly. "I have learned that I can pleasure myself and feel good about it," she said. "When I feel tense, I tell myself 'Masturbate, don't masticate'," she added. "Even though I am heavy and he does reject me, I have to start liking my body and getting enjoyment from it."

Learning to accept and enjoy our bodies, *even when they are not "perfect"* (and whose is?) is what this chapter is all about. Last week we asked you to look at yourself in a full-length mirror and learn to accept and validate your body. What did you discover about the way you looked? How did it feel to look at your body? Which parts of your body did you feel proud of? Which parts did you feel like hiding?

Doris, the attractive, "stacked" brunette, whom we described at the beginning of the chapter, only focused on her negative aspects. When she looked at her attractive face with her huge brown eyes, long hair, sexy tan and even, white teeth, all she saw was her "double chin" when she pressed it against her throat. (We all get double chins when pressing our chin to our throat.) She focused on the one negative area and could not see any attractive features. When she was asked to tell us what she liked about her body starting at the top of her head and going to her toes, she first mentioned her chin and then went down to her waist which she again found too fat. She skipped a great deal of territory between her neck and her waist as well as anything above her chin! Doris, unfortunately, is typical of many women who only focus on their "negative" features and are "blind" to their attractive ones. They "tune out" their good points and do not see themselves the way others see them. Frequently, they also distort what they see.

Carla, a tall, well-proportioned woman, saw herself as having huge, humongous thighs, despite the fact that she was able to get into a small size pair of pants and in spite of what her mirror and others told her. She distorted the way she perceived her thighs, seeing them as abnormally large whereas, in fact, they were in proportion to the rest of her body. When she looked in the mirror, like Doris, she *ignored* the rest of her body and only focused on her imperfections.

Alice also tended to exaggerate how she saw her tummy. Whereas it looked flat to most people, she tended to see it as protruding and ignored her other pretty features, focusing instead on her perceived imperfection. In general, women tended to be very critical of their bodies and applied perfectionistic standards to them, just as they did to other areas of their lives. If they perceived a part of their body as less than perfect, they focused on this "mistake" rather than all their other good features. In fact, they tended to be "blind" to or ignore the parts of their bodies that were attractive. It may be surprising for you to see which parts of your body you may have left out. Study your list of the parts of your body that you like. What parts of your body have you left out? Why? If you find yourself dismissing some parts just because they are "okay" and don't look unusually terrible in your opinion, go back and validate those parts.

Many women applied all-or-nothing thinking to their attractive features. If a feature was not totally "perfect," they didn't mention it. For example, Carla realized she had a very pretty smile but did not feel she could call this an attractive feature because her teeth were not even. Joann liked her eyes but felt her eyelashes were too short. A feature does not have to be one hundred percent "perfect" for you to like it or consider it attractive. Learn to say to yourself, "I may not be perfect but parts of me are excellent."

A first step in accepting our bodies is to change our perfection-istic attitudes and thoughts about them. Your body does not have to be perfect before you can like it. Together with that is a change in behavior. Many women, for example, will not buy themselves the clothes they like until they are slim and can get into them. Again, they are waiting to be "perfect" before they can reward themselves. Learn to dress for now and not for when you are slim. By giving your body the proper attention it needs and treating it as though it is worthy of good clothes, you are really saying that you can accept it for now. Learn to wear "thin clothes" even when you weigh more than you want to. Susie Orbach[2] states that it is not a criminal act to tuck in your blouse or shirt when you are overweight. She reports that women have the misconception that loose clothes make them look smaller than fitted ones. Dress as you would if you really liked your figure, and gradually you will start to accept it.

Even if you find it difficult to like most of your body, *behave* as though you do, and you will find that with time you will learn to adjust to it. Many women who do not like their bodies "hide" them in other ways than loose clothing. They slouch, stand behind others and in many ways do not call attention to their bodies. Many report that when they feel thin, they sit, stand and dance quite differently than when they feel heavy. Learn to adopt these open postures you project when thin even when you are feeling heavy.

Learning to like and accept your body may take a long time or it may only take looking at yourself in the mirror several times and learning to "own" all your parts. If you have a great deal of diffi-culty with certain body parts, continue to look at and explore your body in the mirror until you can look at those parts without disgust. Learn also to look at all of your body parts, not only those you don't like, and to highlight those parts of you that are "excellent" even though all of you may not be "perfect."

When you study yourself in the mirror, evaluate yourself using a different criterion than the weight. Many women mistakenly judge their body only in terms of how fat or thin it is without paying attention to other details such as shape, texture or function. Many ignore their facial features completely, forgetting that it is your face that is the first thing others notice about you.

Ask other people what they like about you and your body and learn to see yourself through their eyes rather than your own critical ones. Feedback from others was very important for the women participating in our groups. It was surprising to them that other wo-men did not see them the way they saw themselves. Alice, for

77

example, saw her body as a "rolypoly pear." The group was truly surprised as she was trim, slim and well-proportioned. It was difficult for her to believe their comments at first but she found it easier to do so when she gave feedback to others about their own distortions of their bodies. If others say they like a particular feature of yours, accept it and try to emphasize that feature. Those parts of you that are excellent demand attention and recognition!

What was perhaps most surprising for our group members was what little importance weight played in others' perceptions of attractiveness. Although a slim body contributed to one's attractiveness, other features played a more important role. What was even more noticeable than the attractive physical features were the attractive behaviors. For many women, their smile, their laugh, their way of talking or moving were what others noticed and liked most about them. Donna was surprised to find that her smile was the first thing women mentioned about what made her pretty. She had been so self-conscious about the wrinkles around her mouth when she smiled that she generally kept her mouth closed. Yet her smile was considered her most attractive feature. Diana was complimented on her expressive eyes which were the first thing people noticed about her. Unfortunately, she focused all her attention on her midriff. Attractive behaviors included smiling, laughing, a graceful walk, a sexy voice, among other behaviors that had little to do with either weight or physical features. What are some of your behaviors that others find attractive about you?

As you look at your body, also learn to appreciate it for other than aesthetic purposes. "Most of all, I guess I like my body because it's healthy and it works," said Rhoda. This was echoed in many ways by other women. "I like the fact that I am strong and athletic. I am really well coordinated, and I feel I can protect myself if I need to," added another woman. "I like how my body feels when I run," said a third, "and when I dance. I just like the feel of it." A fourth woman who had reported feeling bothered by her protruding tummy also said that she liked to belly dance and enjoyed her belly because she could move it. Some women said they liked their hands because they were agile. "I like the way my hands look when I play the piano. They move the way I want them to, and they make beautiful music." Others also took pride in their hands because with those hands they could create or write or type.

As you learn to appreciate your body parts for their function rather than only their outer appearance, you may be surprised at what you discover about yourself. Go back to the mirror and talk to each body part about what you appreciate about it. You may, for example, like your hair because it is so manageable and easy to set. Or you may like your eyes because your vision is so good. Or you may even like some body parts for the pleasure they give you. Even though she didn't like the size of her breasts, Doris appreciated them because of the sensual feelings they gave her when they were stroked. Learn to really appreciate your body for the pleasure it gives you and to look at each body part for the purpose it serves rather than the way it looks.

Learn to become friends with your body. It is yours and you have lived in it for a long time. You know it better than anyone else. Would you really feel comfortable in any other body? This is yours, uniquely yours, and there is no other body just like it. Come on, be honest, could you really feel comfortable in anyone else's body but your own?

Becoming comfortable with your body also means learning to see your body realistically without distortions. Learn to see yourself the way you really appear to others rather than the way you "feel" you look. Look at the photo you picked out last week of what you think you look like. Did you show it to your friends? What feedback did you get about it? It has been our experience that most bulimic women have a distorted perception of their bodies and actually see themselves as much fatter than they actually are. Carla, a well-proportioned, trim woman, brought in a picture of an obese woman to represent what she thought she looked like. She actually believed that she looked like the obese woman in the picture. Even though your friends may tell you that you do not look like the photo you brought in, you may not believe them. You may feel they are just "being nice" or trying to make you feel good, just as Alice did when others did not confirm their perception of her as a "rolypoly pear."

How can you tell if your image of your body is accurate or distorted? If you are not willing to take your friends' assessments at face value, maybe you would like to try some reality testing on your own. Stand in front of a wall or mirror or lie down on a large sheet of paper and have a friend trace an outline of your body. Take a ruler and measure the proportions of your body. Write those down. Scale those down to the size of the photo and compare the measurements. This exercise may take some time and involve taking detailed and accurate measurements, but it may be worth the effort to help you get an accurate perception of your body.

Another way is to take a silhouetted photo of yourself in a dark leotard and compare those measurements with those of the photo. Again, this will involve taking accurate measurements and not just subjective scanning. If you like, you can have a friend or your therapist help you with this. Look at the proportions. Those give you the most accurate picture. How accurate is your perception of yourself?

Still another way to check if your body image is realistic is to look at the Weiss Body Image Scale[3] on the next pages. There are ten silhouetted figures with increasing body sizes. Ask your friends to rate you or a photo of yourself on that scale. Now ask them to rate the photo of what you think you look like on that scale. Is there a difference? Or ask them to rate you on the scale and compare that with how you perceive yourself. Learning to accept and like your body starts with seeing it accurately and realistically. Know *what you really look like* as opposed to *what you feel you look like*. If you are like many "thin-fat" people — people who are, in reality, of normal weight but feel fat — this may take some time. But work on this until you learn to see your body realistically and until you can correct your distortions. If the feedback you receive indicates that you do in fact have a distorted image of your body, learn to *think* of yourself as looking the way you really are, even if you still *feel* fat.

Even if you still "feel" fat or even if you *are* overweight, even by the most objective standards, how big a role does your body play for others? Is thinness the only way to be attractive? How else can you be attractive besides by being thin? What is considered attractive or sexy by others? Look back over your homework. What did you discover when you asked others to tell you whom they considered attractive or sexy? What were your reactions to what you heard? Were you surprised?

"I asked three men whom they considered sexy," said Alice, "and I was really surprised because they all mentioned this woman who is cute but she's also somewhat overweight. She has a pretty face and freckles. I asked them what was physically attractive about her, and they said she had a cute round butt and she's quite 'stacked.' She has a round face and curly hair. I'm really surprised because this woman is 'round' and not a skinny beanpole." Other women were also surprised to see what a small role slimness played in men's perceived attraction of women. Physical features as long hair, expressive eyes, an attractive smile and sensuous movements appeared much more important than weight in whether a woman was judged as attractive or sexy by men. What was even more surprising was that attractiveness to the opposite sex or sexiness was defined most often by other than physical features. Even though physical attractiveness played some role in defining a person as sexy, other intangible qualities were listed more often by both men and women. Even though we frequently give lip service to the saying that "Beauty is only skin deep," many women were surprised to see that was really so in their case.

Take a few minutes to ask yourself what you find sexy or attractive. Think of several people you know and whom you have been attracted to (other than movie stars!). What qualities make

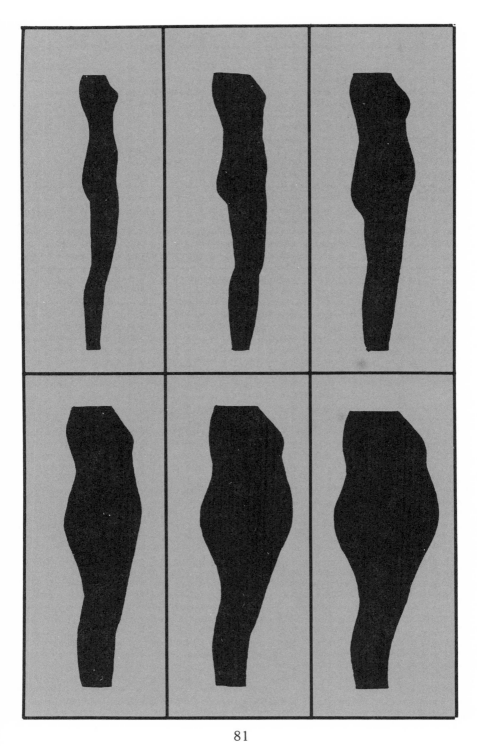

81

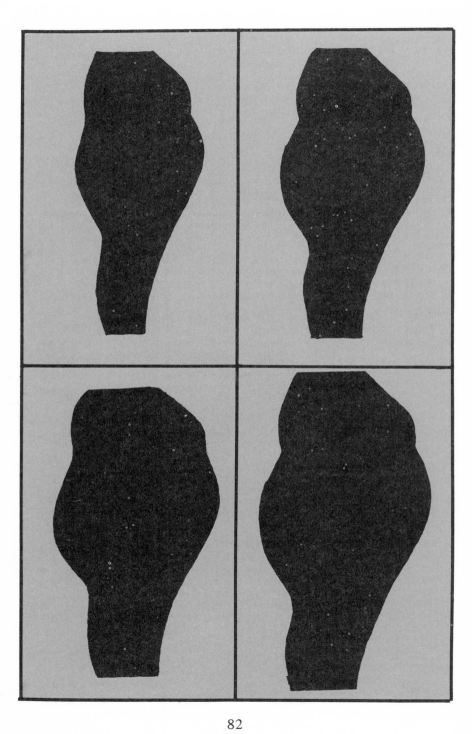

these people attractive? What is sexy for you? If you are like many people, you may know some men and women with "near perfect" features whom you do not find attractive at all or who do not turn you on. You may also know others who are average looking by most external standards but whom you find sexy. What is this intangible quality called sexiness?

"How a man talks to me is very sexy — his voice, his delivery, his sensitivity. It's hard to really define," said one woman. "I know Joe would not be considered handsome but I find him incredibly sexy."

In one of our group sessions, we made a list of what women said they considered sexy in a man.

What Is Sexy?

Bright	Self-confident
In love	Talented
Handsome	Sense of humor
Athletic	Sensitive
Healthy	Musical
A runner	Personality
Kind	Delivery
Considerate	Tan
Caring	Voice
Loving	An individual

They were all surprised to find out how few of the qualities had to do with weight or even with physical appearance. Can you add to this list? What is sexy for you? Write it down.

We hope that through doing these exercises you will learn to like and appreciate your body and become more comfortable with it. You may also become aware that you are more than your body, and that other behaviors contribute as much to your attractiveness to others as weight and physical features.

HOMEWORK

This week we will ask you to do two exercises to help you further enhance your body image and to become aware of the importance of factors other than weight in your attractiveness to others.

1A. Write down what you like about your appearance, what others

83

like about it and list your "attractive behaviors" below.

What I Like About My Appearance

What Others Like About My Appearance

My "Attractive Behaviors"
(How else am I attractive beside being thin?)

1B. Pick one of your "attractive behaviors" from the list and exaggerate it; that is, change something behaviorally that will improve your attractiveness. For example, if people like your smile, smile more often this week. If they like your movements, try exaggerating those. Record reactions from others to this.

2. Change something in your appearance aside from losing weight. Try a new hairstyle, new makeup, wearing earrings, or anything else aside from weight that will make a difference in your appearance. Record reactions from others to this.

3. Continue your binge diary.

NOTES

WEEKLY BINGE DIARY

NAME_____ WEEK NO._____

	TIME	WHAT I ATE	FEELINGS AND THOUGHTS PRIOR TO EATING	ALTERNATIVE COPING SKILLS
MONDAY				
TUESDAY				
WEDNESDAY				
THURSDAY				

WEEKLY BINGE DIARY

NAME_____ WEEK NO._____

	TIME	WHAT I ATE	FEELINGS AND THOUGHTS PRIOR TO EATING	ALTERNATIVE COPING SKILLS
F R I D A Y				
S A T U R D A Y				
S U N D A Y				

TOTAL NUMBER OF BINGES THIS WEEK_____

TOTAL NUMBER OF PURGES THIS WEEK_____

WEEK SEVEN

SUMMING UP: WHERE ARE YOU NOW AND WHERE DO YOU GO FROM HERE?

It is now the last week of the program and time to take stock of what changes you have made so far and what changes you still need to make. We have covered a great deal of material in the last seven weeks. Maybe it is time now to assess what you have gained from the program so far. Write down the answers to these questions.

1. What changes have occurred in my eating habits since I started this program? Please include changes in eating behavior, thoughts and feelings. You may wish to review your answers to the questions in Week One to help you respond to this question and others.

87

2. What other changes have I noticed in myself since the beginning of the program?

3. Has there been an increase, no change or decrease in the following behaviors since I started the program?

	Decrease	No change	Increase
Number of binges	_____	_____	_____
Number of purges after bingeing	_____	_____	_____
Amount of caloric intake with each binge	_____	_____	_____
Length of binge	_____	_____	_____
Eating 3 meals a day	_____	_____	_____
Weighing myself daily	_____	_____	_____
Number of whole days with no binge	_____	_____	_____
Using coping responses other than bingeing	_____	_____	_____

The answers to these questions will help you evaluate your progress so far. To assess where you still need to go, it would be a good idea to go back and review some of the highlights of the program. You will get the most out of this chapter if you refer to your notes in previous chapters and study them slowly and systematically. Reread all or portions of previous chapters.

In the first chapter, we have provided an overview of bulimia — what it is and what it's not. Bulimia unfortunately is not an easy way to lose weight. It has many physical and psychological hazards. We view bulimia as a learned habit rather than as an incurable disease, a habit that you can learn to modify and control. Viewing bulimia as an incurable disease and one over which you have no control is one of the many misconceptions about this behavior. All of these misconceptions about bulimia are really excuses or cop-outs for not taking responsibility for your behavior. Go back to Week One and review your list of cop-outs. Which ones have you stopped using? Which of those do you still use from time to time? Write those down in the space below:

In the second week, we have discussed eating as coping and have tried to help you find alternative ways for you to cope. The first step in changing behavior is identifying those situational and emotional triggers right before you binge. We have said that starvation is frequently a trigger for bingeing. One of the *best preventive measures* for an oncoming binge is to eat three meals a day because *bingeing is one of the physiological consequences of starvation.* Even if you do overeat, *do not purge no matter what.* Knowing that you will be purging afterwards gives you permission to binge. We have provided basic nutritional information to show you that you can maintain your weight by consuming a fairly healthy amount of food. Review the nutritional information and look at your eating habits. Are you eating three meals a day? Have you stopped purging even if you do binge or overeat? Write your answers below. If your eating habits are still sporadic and if you still see purging as a viable means to lose weight, you will need to work on these two basic steps some more.

Now review your binge diary over the past seven weeks to help you further identify your thoughts and feelings prior to bingeing. What are some of the things you tell yourself before you binge? Write those down. What can you do about them?

Reread your list of alternative coping responses as well as the suggestions in the second week for other ways of coping. Which coping responses have you successfully incorporated? Which other ones do you need to use? Write these down.

Now review Week Three and see if perhaps you have learned to be a little easier on yourself. Look at your "shoulds." Are you being just a teeny bit less demanding of yourself? How many more "I wants" are you engaging in? How can you be even nicer to yourself? Write down your responses below.

Review your homework for that week and let yourself feel good again as you read about your positive qualities. Review your list of nourishing activities. Are you still "nourishing" yourself in other ways than food? If you aren't, write down ways that you could be nourishing yourself and giving yourself a treat.

Review your notes on Week Four. Have you noticed a difference in how assertive you are? Are you expressing your anger more readily? Are you saying "no" more often? What do you still need to work on? Write it down.

In Week Five, we discussed some of the societal pressures on women to be thin and to look like the "perfect woman." We hope that you have become aware of the heavy price of trying to attain this impossible goal and are learning to like yourself more, regardless of how much you fall short of this unrealistic image. We also hope to bring to your awareness that attractiveness is based on other qualities than thinness and to help you appreciate those other behaviors in yourself. How do you feel about your body now? Have you become more aware of your attractive behaviors and what others like about you? Is weight playing a less important role in your perception of attractiveness? What do you still need to work on? Write down your responses.

In Week Six, we further discussed learning to like our bodies more and to see ourselves more realistically. What have you learned about how you see yourself? Which parts of your body have you learned to like and accept more? Which parts of your body do you still have a problem with? Write your responses below. Keep looking in the mirror until you feel more comfortable with your body. Continue to exaggerate your "attractive behaviors" and to focus on changing other aspects of your appearance apart from losing weight.

Now go back and reread your notes in this chapter and use them to help you answer the question: What do I still need to work on? If you'd like, you can summarize your answer in the space below.

This workbook is to be used even after the end of the seven week program. In it you have all the tools to help you control your bingeing. Some parts may be more meaningful to you than others. Review this book from time to time. Use it to remind yourself of some skills you have learned. Or if you are having a particular problem, see what has worked for you in the past.

We suggest that you continue filling out your binge diary after the seven weeks are over. We have provided an extra weekly record at the end of this chapter that you may copy to use for the next 45 weeks. We feel a year of monitoring your eating behavior will help make your new habits more ingrained. You may wish to continue recording your eating behavior for even longer than that.

Now, even though you may have changed your eating behavior completely and haven't had a binge in weeks, you may still have relapses from time to time. Expect those — remember, nobody's perfect! What is relapse? It's a binge after you have been *soooo* good! It's an expected event, and when it happens, it is not the end of the world.

Relapse can be your friend. Relapse is a cue to practice your new skills even harder. It gives you a chance to see how strong you really are. Progress seldom goes upwards in a straight line, though it sure would be nice if it did! Progress generally goes up and down, with little dips on the way up. Each little dip is a relapse, a temporary step back, but the end result is success. The little slips will happen. Don't be scared when they do. It's your chance to practice new coping skills, to see how much you have learned and how strong you are. See each relapse as a challenge and as an opportunity to come up with new skills.

What should you do if you have relapses? First of all, don't panic! And *don't — don't — don't* — allow "all-or-nothing" thinking such as "I messed up, it's all over, I knew I couldn't kick the habit." Relapsing does not take away your progress so far. It just means getting up again and resuming your new skills. Maybe your relapse is a cue that you need to nourish yourself more in other ways than food. Be good to yourself. Do something to make yourself feel good, like buy a new shirt (your size hasn't changed from one or two binges).

Have faith in yourself! Don't torture yourself. You're not a bad person if you relapse — you're normal.

In this book we have provided you with some information about bulimia. We view it as a learned habit that can be controlled by understanding the triggers for bingeing and developing new ways of coping. We have presented a program for controlling bulimia based on the research findings that bulimic women are depressed, have perfectionistic tendencies, a high need for approval, difficulty expressing anger and a poor opinion of themselves and their bodies.

Whereas this program has helped many bulimic women, it may not necessarily work for you. If it hasn't helped you, do not feel that you have failed. You may need to see a therapist or join a group. Find a psychotherapist in your community who will help you with this problem. If there is a university in your area, contact the counseling center there for help. Or ask your local Mental Health

Association to refer you to someone.

There are also many national and local organizations that help people with eating disorders. They send information to anyone who requests it and many also offer referrals for therapists. You can write any of these organizations. Most require a stamped, self-addressed envelope.

Anorexia Nervosa and Associated Disorders, Inc.
P. O. Box 271
Highland Park, Illinois 60035

Anorexia Nervosa and Related Eating Disorders, Inc.
P. O. Box 5102
Eugene, Oregon 97405

Associates for Bulimia and Related Disorders
31 West 10th Street
New York, New York 10011

These are only a few of the organizations available. Any one of these will provide you with sources of referral and help. Contact them and find a therapist and/or a group that will help you. Remember, you are not alone, and women with your problem have helped themselves. Good luck to you!

NOTES

WEEKLY BINGE DIARY

NAME_____ WEEK NO._____

	TIME	WHAT I ATE	FEELINGS AND THOUGHTS PRIOR TO EATING	ALTERNATIVE COPING SKILLS
MONDAY				
TUESDAY				
WEDNESDAY				
THURSDAY				

WEEKLY BINGE DIARY

NAME_____ WEEK NO._____

	TIME	WHAT I ATE	FEELINGS AND THOUGHTS PRIOR TO EATING	ALTERNATIVE COPING SKILLS
F R I D A Y				
S A T U R D A Y				
S U N D A Y				

TOTAL NUMBER OF BINGES THIS WEEK_____

TOTAL NUMBER OF PURGES THIS WEEK_____

FOOTNOTES

INTRODUCTION

[1]The Book of the Apocrypha. Ecclesiasticus 31:21.

[2]Diagnostic and statistical manual of mental disorders (3rd ed.), Washington, D.C., American Psychological Association, 1980.

[3]Hilde Bruch, *Eating Disorders: Obesity, anorexia and the person within*. New York: Basic Books.

[4]R. S. Stangler & A. M. Prinz, "DSM-III: Psychiatric diagnosis in a university population," *American Journal of Psychiatry 137*(8) (1980):937-940.

[5]K. A. Halmi, J. R. Falk & E. Schwartz, "Binge eating and vomiting: A survey of a college population," *Psychological Medicine 11* (1981):697-706.

[6]M. Katzman, S. A. Wolchik & S. Braver, "The Prevalence of bulimia and binge eating in a college sample," *International Journal of Eating Disorders*, 3 (1984) 53-62.

[7]R. L. Pyle, J. E. Mitchell & E. D. Eckert, "Bulimia: A report of 34 cases," *Journal of Clinical Psychiatry 42* (2) (1981) 60-64.

[8]C. G. Fairburn & P. J. Cooper, "Self-induced vomiting and bulimia nervosa: An undetected problem," *British Medical Journal 284* (1982) 1153-1155.

[9]C. L. Johnson, M. K. Stuckey, L. D. Lewis & D. M. Schwartz, "Bulimia: A descriptive survey of 316 cases," *International Journal of Eating Disorders, 2* (1982) 3-16.

[10]M. A. Katzman & S. A. Wolchik, "Behavioral and emotional antecedents and consequences of binge eating in college women," Presented at Eastern Psychological Assn., Philadelphia, PA, 1983.

[11]G. R. Leon, K. Carroll, B. Chernyk & S. Finn, "Binge eating and associated habit patterns within college student and identified bulimic populations," *International Journal of Eating Disorders* 4 (1985) 43-47.

[12]S. C. Wooley & O. W. Wooley, "Overeating as substance abuse," in N. Mello (ed.) *Advances in Substance Abuse*, Vol. 2 (1981) 41-67, Greenwich, CT: JAI Press.

13G. F. M. Russell, "Bulimia nervosa: An ominous variant of anorexia nervosa," *Psychological Medicine 9* (1979) 429-448.

14J. E. Mitchell, R. L. Pyle & E. D. Eckert, "Frequency and duration of binge-eating episodes in patients with bulimia," *American Journal of Psychiatry 138* (6) (1981) 835-836.

15D. Herzog, "Bulimia: The secretive syndrome," *Psychosomatics 23* (1982) 481-483, 487.

16S. F. Abraham & P. J. V. Beumont. "How patients describe bulimia or binge eating." *Psychological Medicine 12* (1982) 625-635.

17M. Boskind-Lodahl & W. C. White, *Bulimarexia: The binge-purge cycle* NY: W. W. Norton & Co., (1983) pp. 130-143.

18C. Fairburn, "A cognitive behavioral approach to the treatment of bulimia," *Psychological Medicine 11* (1981) 707-711.

19J. Rosen & H. Leitenberg, "Bulimia nervosa: Treatment with exposure and response prevention," *Behavior Therapy 13* (1982) 117-124.

20M. A. Katzman & S. A. Wolchik, "Bulimia and binge eating in college women: A comparison of personality and behavioral characteristics," *Journal of Consulting and Clinical Psychology*, 52 (1984) 423-428.

21M. Boskind-Lodahl, "Cinderella's stepsisters: A feminist perspective on anorexia nervosa and bulimia," *Signs' Journal of Women in Culture and Society 2* (1976) 342-356.

22R. C. Hawkins & P. F. Clement, "Binge eating: Measurement problems and a conceptual model," in R. C. Hawkins II, W. Fremouw & P. F. Clement (eds.), *The Binge-Purge Syndrome: Theory, Research and Treatment* (NY: Springer), (1984).

23S. F. Abraham & P. J. V. Beumont, "How patients describe bulimia or binge eating," *Psychological Medicine 12* (1982) 625-635.

24M. A. Katzman & S. A. Wolchik, "Behavioral and emotional antecedents and consequences of binge eating in college women," Presented at Eastern Psychological Assn., Philadelphia, PA, 1983.

25G. R. Leon, K. Carroll, B. Chernyk & S. Finn, "Binge eating and associated habit patterns within college student and identified bulimic populations," *International Journal of Eating Disorders 4* (1985) 43-47.

26R. L. Pyle, J. E. Mitchell & E. D. Eckert, "Bulimia: A report of 34 cases," *Journal of Clinical Psychiatry 42* (1981) 60-64.

27M. Boskind-Lodahl, "Cinderella's stepsisters: A feminist perspective on anorexia nervosa and bulimia," *Signs' Journal of Women in Culture and Society 2* (1976) 342-356.

28M. A. Katzman & L. Weiss, "A multifaceted group treatment of bulimia," Presented at Western Psychological Association, Los Angeles, CA, 1984.

WEEK TWO
Eating as Coping: Developing Alternative Coping Strategies
[1]Julia Child, as quoted in *Cosmopolitan*, December 1983, p. 182.

[2]Metropolitan Life Insurance Company of New York: New Weight Standards for Males and Females (New York: Author, 1983)

[3]Modified from Donald Tubesing's *Stress Skills*, Workshop held in Phoenix, Arizona, 1978.

WEEK THREE
Self-esteem, Perfectionism and Depression
[1]Hattie R. Rosenthal, *Aphorisms* (Hallendale: First Printing Corp., 1980)

[2]D. D. Burns, "The perfectionists' script for self-defeat," *Psychology Today*, November 1980, 34-52.

WEEK FOUR
Anger and Assertiveness
[1]R. E. Alberti & M. L. Emmons, *Your Perfect Right: A Guide to Assertive Behavior* (San Luis Obispo: Impact, 1970)

[2]Manuel J. Smith, *When I Say No, I Feel Guilty* (New York: Dial Press, 1975)

[3]Lonnie Barbach, *For Yourself: The Fulfillment of Female Sexuality* (New York: Doubelday & Co., 1975), pp. 43-44.

WEEK FIVE
Cultural Expectations of Thinness for Women
[1]Susie Orbach, *Fat is a Feminist Issue* (New York: Paddington Press, 1978), pp. 20-21.

[2]Lonnie Barbach, *For Yourself: The Fulfillment of Female Sexuality* (New York: Doubelday & Co., 1975), pp. 46-48.

WEEK SIX
Enhancing Body Image
[1]Tom Burke, "The Crazed Joy of Joan Rivers," *Cosmopolitan*, September 1983, p. 237

[2]Susie Orbach, *Fat is a Feminist Issue* (New York: Paddington Press, 1978), p. 95.

[3]B. Weiss, "Obesity, race and the process-reactive model," Unpublished doctoral dissertation, State University of New York at Buffalo, 1969, pp. 186-188.

BIBLIOGRAPHY

Abraham, S. F. & P. J. V. Beumont, "How patients describe bulimia or binge eating," *Psychological Medicine 12* (1982) 625-635.

Alberti, R. E. and M. L. Emmons, *Your Perfect Right: A Guide to Assertive Behavior* (San Luis Obispo: Impact, 1970).

Barbach, Lonnie, *For Yourself: The Fulfillment of Female Sexuality* (New York: Doubeday & Co., 1975)

Boskind-Lodahl, M., "Cinderella's stepsisters: A feminist perspective on anorexia nervosa and bulimia," *Signs' Journal of Women in Culture and Society 2* (1976) 342-356.

Boskind-Lodahl, M. and W. C. White, *Bulimarexia: The binge-purge cycle* (New York: W. W. Norton & Co., 1983).

Burch, Hilde, *Eating Disorders: Obesity, anorexia nervosa and the person within.* (New York: Basic Books, 1973).

Burns, D. D., "The perfectionists' script for self-defeat," *Psychology Today*, November 1980, 34-52.

Diagnostic and statistical manual of mental disorders (3rd ed.), Washington, D. C., American Psychological Association, 1980.

Fairburn, C., "A cognitive behavioral approach to the treatment of bulimia," *Psychological Medicine 11* (1981) 707-711.

Fairburn, C. G. & P. J. Cooper, "Self-induced vomiting and bulimia nervosa: An undetected problem" *British Medical Journal 284* (1982) 1153-1155.

Halmi, K. A., J. R. Falk & E. Schwartz, "Binge eating and vomiting: A survey of a college population," *Psychological Medicine 11* (1981) 697-706.

Hawkins, R. C. & P. F. Clement, "Binge eating syndrome: Measurement problems and a conceptual model," in R. C. Hawkins, II, W. Fremouw & P. F. Clement (eds.), *The Binge-Purge Syndrome: Theory, Research and Treatment* (New York: Springer, 1984).

Herzog, D., "Bulimia: The secretive syndrome," *Psychosomatics 23* (1982) 481-483, 487.

Johnson, C. L., M. K. Stuckey, L. D. Lewis & D. M. Schwartz, "Bulimia: A descriptive survey of 316 cases," *International Journal of Eating Disorders 2* (1982) 3-16.

Katzman, M. A. & L. Weiss, "A multifaceted group treatment of bulimia," Presented at Western Psychological Association, Los Angeles, CA., 1984.

Katzman, M. A. & S. A. Wolchik, "Behavioral and emotional antecedents and consequences of binge eating in college women," Presented at Eastern Psychological Association, Philadelphia, PA., 1983.

Katzman, M. A. & S. A. Wolchik, "Bulimia and binge eating in college women: A comparison of personality and behavioral characteristics," *Journal of Consulting and Clinical Psychology*, 52 (1984) 423-428.

Katzman, M., S. A. Wolchik & S. Braver, "The prevalence of bulimia and binge eating in a college sample," *International Journal of Eating Disorders*, 3 (1984) 53-62.

Leon, G. R., K. Carroll, B. Chernyk & S. Finn, "Binge eating and associated habit patterns within college student and identified bulimic populations," *International Journal of Eating Disorders* 4 (1985) 43-47.

Metropolitan Life Insurance Company of New York: New Weight Standards for Males and Females, (New York: Author, 1983).

Mitchell, J. E., R. L. Pyle & E. D. Eckert, "Frequency and duration of binge-eating episodes in patients with bulimia," *American Journal of Psychiatry 138* (1981) 835-836.

Orbach, Susie, *Fat is a Feminist Issue* (New York: Paddington Press, 1978).

Rosen, J. & H. Leitenberg, "Bulimia nervosa: Treatment with exposure and response prevention," *Behavior Therapy 13* (1982) 117-124.

Rosenthal, Hattie R., *Aphorisms* (Hallendale: First Printing Corp., 1980).

Russell, G. F. M., "Bulimia nervosa: An ominous variant of anorexia nervosa," *Psychological Medicine 9* (1979) 429-448.

Smith, Manuel J., *When I Say No, I Feel Guilty* (New York: Dial Press, 1975).

Stangler, R. S. & A. M. Prinz, "DSM-III: Psychiatric diagnosis in a university population," *American Journal of Psychiatry 137* (1980):937-940.

Weiss, B., "Obesity, race and the process-reactive model," Unpublished dissertation, State University of New York at Buffalo, 1969, pp. 186-188.

Wooley, S. C. & O. W. Wooley, "Overeating as substance abuse, ' In N. Mello (ed.) *Advances in Substance Abuse* Vol. 2 (1981) 41-67. Greenwich, Connecticut: JAI Press.

ABOUT THE AUTHORS

Lillie Weiss received her Ph.D. in clinical psychology at the State University of New York at Buffalo. She is the former director of the Eating Disorders Program at Good Samaritan Medical Center and an adjunct Associate professor in the Department of Psychology at Arizona State University. Melanie Katzman received her Ph.D. in clinical psychology at Arizona State University. Currently, she is a post-doctoral fellow at the New York Hospital, Cornell Medical Center — Westchester Division and works at the Institute of Behavior Therapy in New York City. Sharlene Wolchik received her Ph.D. in clinical psychology at Rutgers University. She is an Associate professor in the Department of Psychology at Arizona State University. They have been working with bulimic women for several years and have done a great deal of research in the area. They are the co-authors of *Treating Bulimia: A Psychoeducational Approach* and of several articles in the area.